101 WRITING PROMPTS FOR TEENS

STORY STARTERS TO SPARK CREATIVE WRITING - FOR TEENS 13 TO 18

JEFFREY C. CHAPMAN

CONTENTS

INTRODUCTION

Hello and welcome to "101 Writing Prompts for Teens," a wonderful collection of story ideas for you to explore your creativity and imagination. The only thing that limits this book is your imagination. It's more than just a list of writing tasks.

There are 101 carefully thought-out writing ideas inside that cover a wide range of topics, from fantasy to adventure to mystery and more. Each prompt is an idea for where to begin, a way to spark your mind and keep your creative engine going. Through these pages, you'll find talking animals, magical countries, adventures that take you back in time, and a lot more.

"101 Writing Prompts for Teens" isn't just about getting teens to be creative, though. It's also about getting better at writing, learning new words, and getting the courage to share your own stories. This book is an ode to creativity, a play area for teens' thoughts, and proof of the power of words. So get your pen, computer or tablet, clear your mind, and get ready for a creative writing journey you'll never forget

PLEASE CONSIDER LEAVING A REVIEW

Hello there!

As an author, I know just how important reviews are for getting the word out about my work. When readers leave a review on Amazon or any other book stores, it helps others discover my book and decide whether it's right for them.

Plus, it gives me valuable feedback on what readers enjoyed and what they didn't.

So if you've read my book and enjoyed it, I would really appreciate it if you took a moment to leave a review on Amazon. It doesn't have to be long or complicated - just a few words about what you thought of the book would be incredibly helpful.

Thank you so much for your support!

Jeff

CHAPTER 1

DISCOVERING THE HIDDEN TALENT

Objective:

WRITE A STORY WHERE the main character learns a secret skill that changes their life in a big way.

Guidelines:

1. Character Background:

- Make sure your main character is balanced. Describe what they do every day, such as their job, hobbies, and friends. They might feel like their lives are missing something or that they haven't reached their full potential yet.

2. Talent Discovery:

- Put the character in a situation where they can discover their talent. It could have been something they found by accident while under a lot of stress, a hobby they never really got into, or a skill they didn't know they had. They should be just as shocked by the discovery as everyone else.

3. Exploration and Impact:

- Describe the character's path to learning this new skill. How can they make it better and accept it? Show how this talent changes their daily life, such as how it helps them get more attention, how it changes their career path, or how it changes the way they interact with other people.

4. Challenges and Growth:

○ Describe the problems the character has to deal with because of their talent. This could be because of other people's jealousy, their own doubts about themselves, or the fact that they have to balance their new skill with their regular life. Describe how getting through these problems helps them grow as people.

5. Conclusion:

○ Finally, talk about how the character's life has changed since they found their talent. Think about how self-aware they are now and how they see the future. Maybe they have a new purpose, more confidence, or opportunities they hadn't thought of before.

CHAPTER 2

A WORLD OF COLORFUL EMOTIONS

Objective:

W RITE A NARRATIVE SET in a world where people's emotions are visibly displayed by the color of their auras, and describe how this affects a day in this world.

Guidelines:

1. **World-Building:**

   - Set the stage for your world. How exactly do these auras work? Do certain colors correspond to specific emotions? Consider how this phenomenon has impacted society's daily life, communication, and culture.

2. **Main Character:**

   - Introduce a character who is navigating this world. How do they feel about their emotions being visible to all? What color is their aura typically, and what does it reveal about them?

3. **Daily Life Interaction:**

   - Describe your character's typical day. How do they interact with others while everyone's emotions are on display? Show a variety of interactions, including those with family, friends, coworkers or students, and strangers.

4. Impact of Visible Emotions:

- ○ Discover how visible auras affect social interactions and relationships. Are people more empathetic, or are there more conflicts? How does the character's behavior change based on the colors they see in others?

5. Specific Scenarios:

- ○ Create specific scenarios that show the impact of these auras. This could include a misinterpretation of an aura, an unexpected connection with someone due to compatible aura colors, or a situation in which someone tries to hide or change their aura color.

6. Reflection on Emotion and Communication:

- ○ Use your narrative to consider the larger implications of such a world. How does this visibility affect emotional honesty, privacy, and interpersonal relationships? Are people more or less likely to express their true feelings?

7. Climactic Event:

- ○ Include a dramatic event that either challenges or highlights your world's uniqueness. This could be your character's personal crisis, a public event, or a significant interaction influenced heavily by aura color.

8. Conclusion:

- ○ Wrap up your story by reflecting on what this day reveals about your character and their surroundings. How does living in a world with visible emotions influence their perception of themselves and others?

CHAPTER 3

THE HEIRLOOM'S SECRET

Objective:

WRITE A STORY ABOUT a family heirloom that has a mysterious past. Show how it has affected the present and what that history is.

Guidelines:

1. **Heirloom Description:**

   o Begin by giving a detailed description of the heirloom. What kind of thing is it? Think about how old it is, how it looks, and if it has any special traits that could lead you to its mysterious past.

2. **Family Background:**

   o Tell us about the family that has the heirloom. Tell us about their relationship with the object and any stories or legends that go along with it. Does the family love it, fear it, or not care about it?

3. **Main Character and Connection to the Heirloom:**

   o Pay attention to a family member who is very interested in or affected by the heirloom. Find out how they first felt about the object and what interested them about it.

4. **Discovery of the Mystery:**

○ Describe how the main character starts to figure out what the heirloom is hiding. To do this, you might have to look for hidden compartments, old letters, or other clues that help you figure out its history.

5. The Heirloom's Past Revealed:

○ Slowly show the heirloom's mysterious past. Did it have anything to do with history, a long-lost family member, or something supernatural?

6. Impact on the Present:

○ Show how finding out about the heirloom's past history changes things for the family now. In what ways does it change their view of their heritage, solve a family mystery, or bring them together or further apart?

7. Character's Personal Journey:

○ Find out how the discovery changes the main character's path in life. Do they connect with their ancestors, feel like they belong, or find a way to settle personal issues?

8. Climax Involving the Heirloom:

○ Build up to a big moment that has to do with the heirloom. This could be a choice about its future, an explanation of what it really is, or a big event caused by its past.

9. Resolution and Reflection:

○ Finish the story by figuring out the problems and mysteries that were introduced. Think about how the heirloom will help the family understand their past and how it will affect their future.

CHAPTER 4

A DAY IN 2124

Objective:

C REATE A NARRATIVE THAT explores a day in the life of a character living 100 years in the future, showcasing futuristic elements and societal changes.

Guidelines:

1. **Futuristic Setting**:

   o Begin by envisioning the world 100 years from now. How have technology, the environment, and daily living evolved? Describe the general atmosphere and landscape of this future world.

2. **Character Introduction**:

   o Introduce your main character. Consider their occupation, lifestyle, and the role they play in this future society. What are their daily challenges and joys in this advanced era?

3. **Typical Day's Outline**:

   o Describe a typical day for your character. Start from their morning routine - how do they get ready, what kind of technology do they use, and how do they interact with their environment and other people?

4. **Advanced Technology and Society**:

- Incorporate elements of advanced technology that are integral to daily life. This might include futuristic transportation, communication, work environments, or home living. How do these advancements affect the character's day?

5. Social and Environmental Changes:

- Address how society has evolved. What are the new social norms, cultural elements, or political landscapes? Have environmental challenges been overcome, or are they more severe?

6. Personal Experiences and Challenges:

- Show how the character navigates their day, including both personal and professional experiences. What kind of challenges do they face in this future world?

7. Interpersonal Relationships:

- Explore the character's interactions with others. How have relationships and social interactions changed in this future setting?

8. Reflect on the Day's Events:

- Conclude with the character reflecting on their day. What insights do they have about living in this future world? How do they feel about the advancements and changes around them?

CHAPTER 5

FACING THE FEAR

Objective:

W RITE A STORY ABOUT a character who faces and gets over a big fear in an interesting and surprising way.

Guidelines:

1. Character Background:

- Describe your main character. Give them a short background that includes their fear. This fear should be big and have an effect on their choices and daily life.

2. Nature of the Fear:

- Describe the fear in great depth. What does it look like in the character's life? What has stopped them or changed the way they act?

3. Inciting Incident:

- Set up an event that forces the character to face their fear. There shouldn't be a way to avoid the fear in this situation.

4. Unexpected Approach to Overcoming Fear:

- Instead of a typical ending, give the character a way they didn't expect to face and get over their fear. This could be a misunderstanding, a fresh look at things, or a discovery made by accident.

5. Character Development Through Challenge:

○ Show how the character changes when they face their fear. What problems do they face and how do they deal with them? Draw attention to their mental and emotional journey.

6. Climactic Moment:

○ Build up to a turning point where the character faces their fear head-on. This climax should be intense and reveal a lot about the character, showing how they've changed.

7. Resolution:

○ Show what happened after the person got over their fear to end the story. In what ways has the character's life changed? Think about their newfound confidence or way of looking at things.

CHAPTER 6

THE KINDNESS LINK

Objective:

W RITE A STORY ABOUT two strangers who become friends after doing something nice for each other out of the blue.

Guidelines:

1. Character Profiles:

- Start the story with two main characters who don't know each other. Give a short background on each person, focusing on their unique personalities and current life situations.

2. Setting the Scene for Kindness:

- Make up a situation in which these two characters meet by chance. This place should be good for talking to each other, like a park, a public event, or on the way to work.

3. Act of Kindness:

- Tell us all about the act of kindness. It should be something simple but meaningful, like helping them with a problem, giving them something they need, or being there for them emotionally when things are tough.

4. Building a Connection:

- Draw attention to their first thoughts and the things they find they have in common.

5. **Development of Friendship**:

- Show how the relationship changes after this first meeting. Include more dates, activities they both enjoy, or acts of kindness that strengthen their relationship.

6. **Impact of Friendship**:

- Find out how this new friendship changes the lives of both characters. What changes or makes them grow because of this relationship?

7. **Climactic Moment**:

- Look into how this new friendship changes the lives of both characters. In what ways do they grow or change because of this relationship?

8. **Conclusion**:

- At the end of the story, think about how important this friendship is. How did a small act of kindness lead to a connection that will last?

CHAPTER 7

THE HIDDEN ORDER OF HIGH SCHOOL

Objective:

C REATE AN INTERESTING STORY about a mysterious high school group that does terrible things and how those bad things effect the group's members and the school as well.

Guidelines:

1. Secret Society Background:

- First, think about the secret society. What is its purpose and how did it come to be at the high school? How many people are in it, and why do they join? Determine their rules, goals, and order of importance.

2. Main Character Involvement:

- Add a main character who gets involved with the community. Someone like this could be a member, a student who learns about it, or someone whose life is directly affected by what it does. Figure out who they are, what motivates them, and how they fit within the group.

3. Setting the School Scene:

- Describe the atmosphere as in high school. How does the society fit into the social structure of the school? Set the mood and stage the story with this setting.

4. Society's Influence and Activities:

- Describe what the secret society does. How do they impact school life and what do they do? Are they doing something good, something bad, or a mix of the two?

5. Conflict and Impact:

- Add conflict that comes from the activities of the society. There could be conflicts for members, effects on people who aren't members, or arguments with school officials.

6. Character Development:

- Show how the main character's engagement in society changes their personal journey. How challenging are things for them? How does it change their relationships and how they experience the outside world?

7. Climax Involving the Society:

- Run up to an important scene that puts the society and its people to the test. This could involve the central character making a big choice, running the risk of being found out, or doing something important.

8. Resolution and Reflection:

- At the end of the story, talk about how society has influenced the characters and the school. How does the story solve the problems it starts with? What has been shown or evolved?

CHAPTER 8

THE CHANGE MAKER

Objective:

WRITE A STORY ABOUT a character who sees an important issue in their community and starts a movement to fix it will help you understand the journey and the impact it has.

Guidelines:

1. **Character Introduction:**

   ○ Bring a main character who care about their community or want things to change. Give a little history on their life, the principles they hold, and what leads them.

2. **Community Problem Identification:**

   ○ Describe the particular problem that needs to be sorted out in the community. This could be about the economy, society, or the environment. Explain what it means to the community and why it's important.

3. **Movement Initiation:**

   ○ Describe what the character does before starting the movement. This could mean getting support, expanding the word, or setting up the first discussion sessions or events.

4. **Building Momentum:**

◦ Show how the movement gets powerful. This can include getting people to help, planning bigger events, dealing with problems, and discovering how the community reacts.

5. Overcoming Challenges:

◦ Add any issues or disputes that the movement and the character have to deal with, like opposition, problems with logistical issues, or disagreements inside the group.

6. Personal and Movement Growth:

◦ Look out into what happens to the character when they lead the movement. Pay attention to how they handle successes and failures, as well as how they grow as people and as leaders.

7. Climactic Event:

◦ Create up to an important situation that will test the movement's resolution or show them where they need to go the following in their mission.

8. Resolution and Impact:

◦ Show what takes place with the movement at the conclusion. What effect has it had on the community challenge? Think about how the community and the character's life have changed over time.

CHAPTER 9

THE ANIMAL WHISPERER

Objective:

W RITE A STORY ABOUT someone who finds out they can talk to animals. Show how this changes their view of the world and the roles they play in it.

Guidelines:

1. Character Introduction:

- Begin by introducing our primary character. Give them one-of-a-kind background and personality. What did they think about animals and nature before they found out they had this ability?

2. Discovery of the Ability:

- Describe how and when the character learns that they can talk to animals. It took place all of a sudden, or did you realize it over time? How do they feel about the newly acquired facts?

3. First Interactions with Animals:

- Describe the character's first interactions with animals. So what do they learn from interacting with each other? How is talking to animals different from talking to people?

4. Changing Perspectives:

○ Show how the character's perceptions on animals, nature, and environmental problems changes as they gain this ability. Do they change the way they see the outside world?

5. Challenges and Conflicts:

○ Set challenges for them that use their new ability. This could be other people's doubts, moral problems, or the weight of having to understand animals' desires and demands.

6. Developing Relationships:

○ Look into the connections the character makes with different animals. What effect do these relationships have on their personal life and decisions?"

7. Climactic Moment:

○ Look through the bonds the character makes with different animals. What effect do these relationships have on their personal life and decisions?"

8. Resolution and Reflection:

○ At the end of the story, think about how the character's life and outlook have changed. How have they changed the way they think about or experience about the natural world?

CHAPTER 10

THE MESSAGE IN THE BOTTLE

Objective:

W RITE AN INTERESTING TALE about a character on the beach who finds a mysterious message in a bottle and how this leads to a journey or to a surprise that they didn't expect.

Guidelines:

1. **Setting and Character Introduction:**

   - Start by describing thoroughly the beach where the story takes place. Set up details regarding your main character's life and personality. Why do they have to be at the beach today?

2. **Discovery of the Bottle:**

   - Describe the scene when the character finds the bottle. Point out their interest and initial reactions. How does the bottle look and stand out?

3. **Revealing the Message:**

   - Describe the character's experience opening the bottle and reading the message. What's written on it? Is it request for assistance, a mysterious puzzle, a path, or something else entirely?

4. Impact of the Message:

○ Show how the message impacts the character. Does it excite their interest, scare them, or inspire them to react? Is it related to their personal history or their present scenario in any way?

5. Following the Clues:

○ If the message contains a mystery or a quest, explain how the character decides to take on it. Which indications do they follow, and what challenges do they face along the way?

6. Interaction with Other Characters:

○ Introduce more characters who participate in the story, whether they are helpers, obstacles, or have a personal connection to the message.

7. Climactic Discovery or Event:

○ Prepare for an important phase in the message's development. This could include discovering a secret, finding a treasure, meeting someone important, or speaking to a new understanding.

8. Resolution and Reflection:

○ Finish the story by solving the mystery of the message. Consider how this adventure influenced the individual or their life.

CHAPTER 11

THE LIVING SHADOWS

Objective:

C REATE AN IMAGINATIVE TALE set in a world where shadows are sentient entities, looking into the relationships between the shadows and their real-life counterparts.

Guidelines:

1. World-Building:

- ○ Write a detailed description of this fantasy world. How do living shadows coexist among their physical counterparts? Are they visible to everyone? Do they have their own social system or hierarchy?

2. Main Character Introduction:

- ○ Introduce a protagonist having a unique relationship or connection to their shadow. What separates them in a world where everyone casts a living shadow?

3. Nature of the Shadows:

- ○ Describe some of the characteristics of the shadows. Do they share the same personality as the people around them, or do they have totally different attributes? How do they connect and communicate with the physical world?

4. Conflict Involving Shadows:

- Create a central conflict involving the living shadows. This could be a personal conflict, a societal issue, or a threat regarding the balancing between the shadows and the physical world.

5. Adventure or Quest:

- If it suits for your story, send the character on a quest or adventure in the world of shadows. What do they hope to accomplish or discover?

6. Relationship Dynamics:

- Explore the relationship between the lead character and the shadowy character. How does this relationship develop throughout the story? Are moments of harmony, trouble, or a revelation?

7. Climactic Event:

- Develop to a conclusion that tests the character's bond with their shadow or challenges the rules of this fantasy world.

8. Resolution and Reflection:

- Complete with a resolution to the central dilemma. Consider the impact of the story's events on the world and the characters.

CHAPTER 12

THE PRICE OF TELEPORTATION

Objective:

C REATE A SCIENCE FICTION story that takes place in a future where teleportation is possible but has big expenses or consequences.

Guidelines:

1. Futuristic Setting:

- Create a clear representation of the future world in which teleportation technology exist. What does society look like, and how has teleportation impacted daily life?

2. Nature of Teleportation:

- Explain the teleportation technology and method of operation. What are the limitations and risks? What is the 'cost' associated with it, assuming physical, psychological, social, or something else?

3. Main Character Introduction:

- Introduce a main character who can be impacted or involved in teleportation. Do they work in the industry, are they regular users, or have they been impacted by the technology's consequences?

4. Conflict Related to Teleportation:

- Create a central issue about the cost of teleportation. This could include personal loss, social problems, legal issues, or undesirable effects of the technology.

5. Personal and Social Implications:

- Examine both the personal impact on the character and the larger social implications of teleportation. How does technology impact relationships, work, and society?

6. Adventure or Investigation:

- Based on the direction of your story, involve the character in an adventure, mystery, or mission dealing with teleportation challenges.

7. Climactic Confrontation:

- Develop to a final scene that forces the character to confront the central conflict, whether it is a personal challenge or a wider social issue.

8. Resolution and Consequences:

- Complete the story by resolving the conflict. Consider the long-term effects of teleportation on the character's life and the world.

CHAPTER 13

THE LETTER OF MYSTERIES

Objective:

W RITE A SUSPENSEFUL STORY where the main lead receives a cryptic letter, driving to an unexpected and thrilling adventure.

Guidelines:

1. **Intriguing Introduction**:

   ○ Start off by setting the scene and introducing the main hero. Set up their normal lives before the mysterious letter arrives.

2. **The Mysterious Letter**:

   ○ Describe the moment when the character receives the letter. Describe its unique characteristics such as unusual handwriting, strange symbols, or an unfamiliar message that attracts curiosity and suggests adventure.

3. **The Call to Adventure**:

   ○ Let the letter's content look like a call to action. It could be a riddle to solve, a request for assistance, or a clue to a more massive mystery. Why does the character decide to follow up on the letter?

4. **Gathering Clues**:

   ○ As the character begins on their adventure, set a trail of clues for them to follow. These should be interesting and challenging, taking the character to new places or encounters.

5. Introducing Supporting Characters:

- Bring some secondary characters who help or hinder the protagonist's journey. These could be allies, subjects, or adversaries, each with their own motives.

6. Building Tension and Conflict:

- Increase the level of conflict and suspense. As they get closer to solving the mystery, the character may encounter obstacles, red herrings, and possibly dangers.

7. Climactic Discovery:

- Lead up to a dramatic moment when the central mystery of the letter is revealed. This should be both surprising and satisfying, combining the clues and challenges discovered.

8. Resolution and Reflection:

- Finish the story by resolving any secondary plotlines and reflecting on how the adventure has influenced the character's perception of the world.

CHAPTER 14

MISUNDERSTOOD BEGINNINGS

Objective:

C REATE A ROMANTIC STORY where a misunderstanding brings about the initial connection between two characters, leading to an evolving relationship.

Guidelines:

1. Setting the Stage:

- Start by describing the situation in which the initial misunderstanding happens. This could be a social gathering, a workplace, or something unexpected in everyday life.

2. Character Introduction:

- Introduce two main characters, who are destined for romance. Provide some history about each character, emphasizing their personalities, lifestyles, and current relationship status.

3. The Misunderstanding:

- Describe the incident or conversation that resulted in the misunderstanding. Ensure that it is convincing and has the potential to cause conflict or tension between the characters.

4. Initial Reactions:

- Describe each character responds to the misunderstanding. This reaction, whether annoyed, amused, or unaware, should set the tone for their initial relationship.

5. Developing Interaction:

- Show how the characters' interactions continue after the misunderstanding. What events keep bringing them together? How do they begin to perceive each other differently?

6. Deepening Connection:

- As the story progresses, the characters develop a stronger attraction and understanding for each other. Include moments that challenge their initial impressions and reveal deeper compatibility.

7. Conflict and Resolution:

- Introduce a conflict or turning point related to the original misunderstanding or other aspects of their relationship. How do they overcome this challenge?

8. Climactic Romantic Moment:

- Build up to a dramatic romantic moment or realization that strengthens their relationship. This should be a satisfactory conclusion to their emotional journey.

9. Conclusion and Reflection:

- Complete the story with the characters reflecting on their journey from misunderstanding to love. Highlight how their relationship has affected them.

CHAPTER 15

ENTREPRENEURIAL DREAMS

Objective:

W RITE A STORY ABOUT a teenager who builds a unique and innovative small business, exploring the challenges and achievements they face along the way.

Guidelines:

1. **Character Development:**

   o Introduce your teenage protagonist. Give them individual personalities, backgrounds, and motivations. What motivated them to start a business?

2. **Concept of the Business:**

   o Describe your unique small business concept. How did the teenager come up with it? What makes it unique or different from other businesses?

3. **Setting Up the Business:**

   o Show the process of starting the business. This can include brainstorming, planning, gathering resources, and overcoming initial hurdles.

4. **Challenges Faced:**

   o Introduce realistic challenges the teen faces in running their business. This could involve financial issues, balancing school and work, market competition, or skepticism from others.

5. Character Growth and Business Development:

- As the story progresses, show how the business helps the teen's personal development. How do they evolve as individuals and entrepreneurs?

6. Support System:

- Add characters who encourage or mentor the teen on their entrepreneurial journey, such as family, friends, or community members.

7. Climactic Event:

- Build to a pivotal moment in the company's history, such as a major transaction, a critical review, a large sale, or a significant setback.

8. Resolution and Reflection:

- Finish by resolving the major business challenges. Consider what the teen has learned and how they see the future of their business.

CHAPTER 16

ECHOES OF ANCIENT ROME

Objective:

C REATE A STORY SET in ancient Rome and told from the perspective of a young apprentice learning a trade or skill, all while exploring the historical context and daily life of the time.

Guidelines:

1. **Historical Setting**:

   ○ Begin by expressing the setting in ancient Rome. Include details about the city's architecture, social structure, and standard of living to help the reader acknowledge the time period.

2. **Apprentice Character Introduction**:

   ○ Introduce the young apprentice. Provide information about their background, family, and how they became an apprentice. Which trade or skill are they learning?

3. **Master-Apprentice Relationship**:

   ○ Describe the connection between the apprentice and the master. What is the relationship like? Is it strict and formal, encouraging and mentor-like, or something else?

4. Daily Life and Learning:

- ○ Describe a typical day in the life of an apprentice. What are their specific tasks and responsibilities? How do they interact with their colleagues and customers?

5. Historical Events or Elements:

- ○ Include historical events or elements relevant to the time period. How will these events influence the apprentice's life and the world around them?

6. Personal Growth and Challenges:

- ○ Show the apprentice facing challenges associated to their trade, social status, or personal goals. How do these challenges help them grow?

7. Incorporating Historical Figures or Events:

- ○ If appropriate, include interactions with historical figures or participation in significant events from the era to provide a unique perspective on widely recognized aspects of ancient Rome.

8. Climactic Moment:

- ○ Lead to an important moment in the apprentice's journey. This could be a personal accomplishment, a turning point in their apprenticeship, or a significant episode in history that they witness.

9. Resolution and Reflection:

- ○ Complete the story by resolving the major conflicts. Consider how the apprentice's journey has been formed by their experiences in ancient Rome.

CHAPTER 17

THE CURSED PAGES

Objective:

W RITE A TERRIFYING STORY about a haunted book discovered in a library, describing the strange events and supernatural events that occur as a result of the book.

Guidelines:

1. **Eerie Setting:**

   ○ Begin by creating an atmosphere that intensifies the horror element, such as an old, dark library with a mysterious surroundings. Introduce the library's history and any previous events that may be relevant to the story.

2. **Main Character Introduction:**

   ○ Introduce the main character, who finds or is drawn to the haunted book. This could be a library user, student, or librarian. Summarize their initial interest or suspicion toward the book.

3. **Discovery of the Haunted Book:**

   ○ Discuss how the book was discovered. Describe its appearance, title, and any notable features, such as strange symbols, an eerie aura, or terrifying illustrations.

4. **Unleashing the Haunt:**

○ As the character interacts with the book, starting to introduce strange and eerie events. This could begin subtly, such as whispers from the pages or a sense of being tracked, and gradually increase in intensity.

5. Escalating Supernatural Events:

○ Increase the intensity as the story progresses. The character might experience vivid nightmares, see visions, or encounter evil spirits related to the book.

6. Unraveling the Book's History:

○ Include an additional plot in which the character or others investigate the book's history and origin. What cursed events or dark rituals are linked to it?

7. Climactic Confrontation:

○ Build to a climax featuring a face-to-face encounter with the book's supernatural elements. This could be a struggle of wills, an attempt to destroy the book, or a ritual to end the haunting.

8. Resolution and Aftermath:

○ Finish the story by resolving the haunting, whether by containing, destroying, or recognizing the power of the book. Consider the long-term impact on both the character and the library.

9. Lasting Horror:

○ End with a twist that suggests the horror isn't over, such as the book reappearing on a shelf or another person picking it up, implying an ongoing curse.

CHAPTER 18

THE QUEST FOR THE LOST CITY

Objective:

D EVELOP AN EXCITING ADVENTURE story about a quest in search of a legendary lost city, complete with challenges, discoveries, and unexpected twists.

Guidelines:

1. **Intriguing Introduction**:

   ○ Start by setting up a scene for the adventure. Introduce the legend of the lost city – its history, myths, and why it captured explorers and historians. What treasures, knowledge, or secrets is it said to be kept?

2. **Diverse Team of Characters**:

   ○ Assemble a team of characters before starting on the quest. They could be an archaeologist, a thrill-seeking adventurer, a local guide, or a scholar. Give each character a unique personality and reason for joining the quest.

3. **Preparation and Journey Commencement**:

   ○ Summarize the preparation phase, in which the team collects information, maps, and supplies. Describe the first part of the journey, setting up the tone for the adventure.

4. **Challenges and Obstacles**:

- ○ Introduce various obstacles for the team to overcome as they approach the lost city. These could include natural barriers, puzzles, hostile environments, or rivals looking to use the city for their own benefit.

5. **Cultural and Historical Discoveries**:

- ○ Allow the team to discover information about the lost city and its people as they travel. This can include identifying ancient symbols, learning about local traditions, or discovering artifacts of a lost civilization.

6. **Climactic Discovery**:

- ○ Lead up to the discovery of the lost city. Describe the city in full detail, capturing its unique architecture, historical artifacts, and any traces of its inhabitants.

7. **The Twist or Revelation**:

- ○ Once the city is discovered, add an unexpected turn or significant surprise. This could be a hidden truth about the city's history, a surprising connection to one of the characters, or an unexpected challenge that tests the team's talents.

8. **Resolution and Return**:

- ○ Continue the story by accomplishing the main quest. How does the discovery of the lost city impact the characters' understanding of history? What do they choose to do with their exploration?

9. **Reflecting on the Adventure**:

- ○ Put an end to the story by having the characters think about their journey and what they've learned. How has the adventure influenced them, and what new mysteries or questions has developed?

CHAPTER 19

THE REGIME OF EMOTIONS

Objective:

W RITE A DYSTOPIAN STORY set in a world where the government controls emotions, exploring its effects for freedom of speech and society.

Guidelines:

1. **Dystopian World Building:**

   o Establish the dystopian atmosphere. Describe how the government controls emotions, whether through technology, drugs, strict laws, or psychological methods. What is the reason for this power?

2. **Main Character Introduction:**

   o Introduce the main character who lives in this world. How do they initially adapt to or refuse the emotional control? What is their responsibility in this society?

3. **Society Under Control:**

   o Create a picture of what daily life is like under this system of government. How do people interact, work, and live when their emotions are controlled? Show the government's perspective on the benefits and drawbacks that citizens experience.

4. **Awakening and Resistance:**

○ Lead your character to an awaking or realization about the inappropriate or unfair nature of emotional control. What causes this change? It could be an event, a situation, or a personal loss.

5. Building Tension:

○ As the character questions or rebels against the system, highlight the dangers and difficulties they face, like being watched by the government, ignored by society, or finding an underground rebel movement.

6. Conflict with the Regime:

○ Create a conflict between the main character with society or the government. This might involve joining an uprising group, planning a revolt, or informing people the truth about emotional control.

7. Climactic Confrontation:

○ Eventually, the character's struggle to keep their emotions in perspective reaches a climax. This could be a big act of rebellion, a public confession, or a direct clash with the people who are in charge of the rule.

8. Resolution and Reflection:

○ Fulfill the story by figuring out the main issue. What happens because of what the main character does? Think about the state of society and any changes that have occurred.

9. Themes and Messages:

○ Discuss topics like how important it is to have emotional freedom, the effects of dictatorship, and how strong the human spirit is.

CHAPTER 20

A SERIES OF UNFORTUNATE, HILARIOUS EVENTS

Objective:

M AKE A FUNNY STORY about a character's day in which a series of hilarious-bad things happen, leading to laughter and surprising results.

Guidelines:

1. **Comical Introduction:**

   ○ Start by giving an enjoyable introduction to the main character. Without anything going wrong, find out what their normal day-to-day life is like.

2. **First Mishap:**

   ○ Start a series of bad luck with something minor but funny, like someone dropping coffee on themselves, missing the bus, or sending a text message that wasn't understood. This should set off a chain of events that will happen throughout the day.

3. **Escalating Misfortunes:**

   ○ The accidents should happen more often and in more ridiculous ways as the day goes on. This could be a normal situation that gets out of hand or something completely strange happening. Consider humorous and fun things to say.

4. Interaction with Other Characters:

o Adding extra characters who make things more entertaining, whether on purpose or by accident, is important. These people could be family, coworkers, or even strangers.

5. The Peak of Chaos:

o Develop to a climax where several amusing misfortunes meet. Here should be the silliest and funniest part of the story.

6. Turning Point:

o Include a turning point where the character either takes back control of the situation or finds a funny way to deal with it.

7. Resolution with a Twist:

o Make the story ending by tying up all the loose ends from the day's events, but leave room for one last, surprising turn that hints the character's problems may not be over yet.

8. Reflection and Humor:

o At the end, have the character think about the day with humor and a lighthearted attitude. What, if anything, have they learned from all of their occurrences?

CHAPTER 21

SEASONS THROUGH UNSEEN EYE

Objective:

W RITE A POEM ABOUT the changing seasons that tells the story from a different or uncommon point of view.

Guidelines:

1. **Choosing the Perspective:**

   ○ For your poem, choose a narrator that is more unusual. Like a tree or a park bench, this could be a nonliving thing, an animal, or even a natural element, like a traveling bird or a bear resting.

2. **Characterizing the Narrator:**

   ○ Give your narrator an unusual voice and viewpoint. How do they feel or understand the seasons changing? What unusual concepts do they have to offer?

3. **Describing Each Season:**

   ○ Create verses for every season: summer, fall, winter, and spring. Tell what each season is like and how it changes from the perspective and point of view of your chosen narrator.

4. Use of Imagery and Sensory Details:

- ○ Use vivid language and senses to make the seasons come to life. Pay close attention to the sounds, smells, sights, and feels that the storyteller might feel.

5. Emotional Tone and Theme:

- ○ Set how you feel about the poem. How does your narrator feel regarding the changes? Are they happy about them, sad, reflective, or even not fascinated? What themes come up when you look at the seasons from their viewpoint?

6. Creative Structure:

- ○ Think about how your poem is put together. You could use poetry or a consistent rhyme strategy. Change the length and rhythm of the lines to fit the mood of the season.

7. Concluding Reflection:

- ○ At the end of the poem, add a verse that connects the experiences of all four seasons. What key concept or message does your narrator want to get across about how time goes by and how seasons change?

CHAPTER 22

DIARY FROM ANOTHER DIMENSION

Objective:

W RITE A CHARACTER'S DIARY entries from a parallel universe, showing their daily life, experiences, and thoughts in a world that is both like ours and quite different from it.

Guidelines:

1. Parallel Universe Setting:

○ Determine how the parallel universe is like. How is it comparable to our world and how is it different? Consider about things like natural laws, technology, society, and culture.

2. Diary Writer Characterization:

○ Make your character who is writing the diary more interesting. A unique personality, background, and point of view should be given to them. In this alternate world, how do they spend their days?

3. First Diary Entry - Introduction:

○ Start with an entry that tells us about the character and the world they live in. This entry can set the mood and show what the character's life is like and the world they live in.

4. Daily Life and Events:

- Each entry after the first one should talk about a day or important event in the character's life. Think about how your normal relationships, activities, and experiences might be different in the other universe.

5. Personal Reflections and Emotions:

- Use the character's diary entries to show what they are thinking, feeling, and reflecting on. How do they see the world around them? What do they hope for, fear, and face?

6. Progression of Entries:

- Make sure all of the entries move forward, whether it's the character's feelings changing, their life changing, or their ideas about the universe changing.

7. Incorporating Unique Elements:

- Add things which are only found in the parallel universe that have an effect on the character's life. This could include different events in history, new technologies, or different norms in society.

8. Final Entry - Reflective Conclusion:

- Finish with a final entry that wraps up what the character has been through so far. Think about how their journey has changed them or what they've learned about themselves and the world around them.

CHAPTER 23

CONVERSATIONS AT TOMORROW'S CAFÉ

Objective:

W RITE A SHORT PLAY'S script that takes place in a futuristic café and focuses on how the characters interact with each other in this unique scene. Include elements of future technology and society in the play.

Guidelines:

1. **Setting the Scene:**

   ○ Start by describing the scene in detail. Describe the futuristic café's atmosphere, the technology it uses (such as holographic menus or automated servers), and how it looks in general.

2. **Character Creation:**

   ○ Include a range of characters that hang out at the café. It could be anyone from regulars and employees to first-time visitors. Assign each character a unique personality and history.

3. **Opening Scene:**

   ○ Begin the play with an interesting scene that sets the mood. This could be a character walking into the café, a conversation going on, or something special happening in the café.

4. Dialogue and Interaction:

- Listen to what the characters are saying to each other. What they say to each other can help you figure out who they are, what the future world is like, and what the café does for them.

5. Incorporate Futuristic Elements:

- Bring futuristic ideas into the play without difficulties. This could happen when characters talk about current events in their world, when they use advanced technology, or when they show how people live in the future.

6. Develop the Plot:

- Establish an important issue or plot that drives the play. One character's personal problem, a mystery going on in the café, or big events happening in the community could be the focus of this.

7. Climactic Moment:

- Bring the story to a climax that either ends the main plot or gives the characters some new information or a sudden change.

8. Concluding Scene:

- Finish the play with a scene that rounds up the story. Think about the ideas that were brought up, and then leave the audience with one last thought or question.

9. Stage Directions:

- Provide actors and directors clear stage directions to follow. Describe how the characters move, what they say, and how they interact with the café.

CHAPTER 24

LETTERS TO THE FUTURE

Objective:

W RITE A CHARACTER'S PERSONAL and reflective letter to their future self. In it, they should talk about their hopes, fears, expectations, and questions about the future.

Guidelines:

1. Character Introduction:

- Introduce the person who is writing the letter before beginning. Give some background on their current situation, including their age and any important events or problems they are facing.

2. Tone and Voice:

- Figure out the letter's style. Being hopeful, worried, curious, or a mix of these feelings is what it can be. There should be a clear voice that stays the same throughout the letter for the character.

3. Addressing the Future Self:

- Talk to the character's future self directly. How do they think of themselves in the future? What do they think of having changed in their lives?

4. Current Life Reflections:

- Think about the character's present situation. What do they hope for, fear, and dream about right now? What problems do they have right now?

5. Hopes and Questions for the Future:

- Write down what the character wants for themselves in the future. What do they hope to achieve or grow as a person? Do they have set objectives that they want to achieve?

6. Fears and Uncertainties:

- Write down any worries or fears the character has about the future. What questions do they have about the possible paths their life could take? How do they plan to deal with these?

7. Advice or Wishes:

- What advice would the character give to themselves in the future? Remembering values, lessons learned, or hopes for keeping certain relationships or ideals alive could be part of this.

8. Closing Thoughts:

- Finish the letter with some final thoughts or a touching message. It could be a promise to love themselves again, a note of encouragement about the future, or a reminder of where they've come from.

9. Personal and Emotional Depth:

- Make sure the letter is very personal and emotional, giving you a look into the character's mind and journey.

CHAPTER 25

VOICES OF THE STORY

Objective:

W RITE A SHORT STORY that proceeds entirely through character dialogue, with no explanation, to show the plot, personalities, and feelings of the characters.

Guidelines:

1. **Character Voices:**

   ○ Give each character in the dialogue their own unique voice. Their speech should show who they are, where they come from, and how they feel.

2. **Setting the Scene Through Speech:**

   ○ Help the reader guess the context and era by using the dialogue. Readers can get clues from the characters by looking at their surroundings or the situation they're in.

3. **Unfolding the Plot:**

   ○ Use the characters' conversations to build the plot. It's best for events, conflicts, and new developments to become visible as the characters talk to each other.

4. **Expressing Emotions and Reactions:**

   ○ Show how the characters feel and what they are thinking by how they talk.

Tone, speed, and the words you use can all show how you're feeling.

5. Creating Conflict and Tension:

○ Use disagreements, misunderstandings, or different points of view in the dialogue to create conflict and tension.

6. Advancing the Story:

○ Ensure that every line of dialogue moves the story forward in some way, whether it's by showing more about the characters, adding to the plot, or creating a more emotional setting.

7. Climactic Conversations:

○ Bring the story's main conflict or theme to the forefront in a key conversation that builds up to the climax.

8. Resolution Through Dialogue:

○ End the story with a conversation that either ends up the plot or gives the reader a satisfying sense of completion, even if some things are left unfinished.

9. Natural and Engaging Conversations:

○ Keep things natural and interesting. It needs to sound like real speech while still being short and clear for telling a story.

CHAPTER 26

REWIND THE TALE

Objective:

M AKE UP A STORY that goes backwards by starting with the ending and then gradually showing what happened before that led to how things ended.

Guidelines:

1. Establish the Ending First:

- Begin your story with its final scene or most important event. This should be an important event that normally brings a story to a close, like the end of a conflict, a big secret, or the peak of a character's journey.

2. Reverse Plot Development:

- Each part of the story that comes after the ending should go back in time and show what happened before the ending. It's kind of like taking off the layers of a story.

3. Reveal Causes and Motivations:

- Show the causes and motives behind the events in the last scene as the story goes forward (or backward). How did the characters reach where they were at the beginning?

4. Character Development in Reverse:

- Show character growth from the last time they were seen. Start with the characters at the end of their journey and show them backwards in time to show how they changed and grew the most important things.

5. Maintain Suspense and Interest:

- Even though the story starts with the ending, keep the reader guessing by not revealing some details until later (earlier in the story's timeline). The reader is then interested in finding out how the characters got to the ending.

6. Climactic Moment in a New Light:

- In the middle of your story, show what would normally be the climax in a way that changes how you see the ending. This will give the last scene more depth and understanding.

7. Beginning as the Final Reveal:

- Traditionally, the beginning of the story should come at the end. For the reader to fully understand the journey that led to the ending, this last reveal should be the last piece of the puzzle.

8. Clear Transitions:

- Make sure the reader knows how to move from one part of the backward timeline to the next. To keep things clear, mark time shifts.

CHAPTER 27

RHYME AND REASON

Objective:

WRITE A STORY WHERE the main character always speaks in rhymes. This particular way of speaking will give the character and the story more depth.

Guidelines:

1. **Character Introduction with Rhyming Quirk:**

    o Introduce your main character and make a point of saying that they speak in rhymes. Explain what led to this trait. Is it magical, a habit, or just a part of their personality?

2. **Rhyming Dialogue Integration:**

    o Make sure that the main character's entire speech is written in rhyming couplets or some other form of rhyming words. The rhymes should sound natural and show how the character feels and what they are thinking.

3. **Interactions with Other Characters:**

    o Show how the other characters feel when the main character rhymes. Are they amused, confused, annoyed, or charmed? For relationships and interactions, this can give them deeper meaning.

4. **Narrative and Plot Development:**

- Make the story's plot better. The main character's rhymes can be very important for moving the story along, solving problems, or making new situations.

5. Balancing Rhymes with Story:

- Even though the main character's statements should rhyme, the story should still flow easily. The trick with the rhymes shouldn't take away from the story.

6. Challenges Related to Rhyming:

- Bring in problems or challenges that have to do with the character's rhymes. What does it mean for their life, their goals, or how they interact with other people?

7. Climactic Moment with Rhyming Twist:

- Build up to a point where the rhymes are very important. This could happen because of a clever way to solve a problem, a confusion, or a moment of intense emotion.

8. Resolution and Character Growth:

- Finalize the story by figuring out how to solve the major problems. Think about what the main character has learned or how they have grown, taking into account the way they speak.

9. Rhyme Scheme Consistency:

- Keep the rhyme scheme for the main character's speech unchanged throughout the story to make it flow better and have more impact.

CHAPTER 28

DIGITAL DIALOGUES

Objective:

W RITE A STORY THAT takes place entirely through text messages and emails. Use this modern way of communicating to show the plot, how characters change, and how emotions affect each other.

Guidelines:

1. **Establish Characters and Relationships:**

   ○ Start the story by showing the characters through the digital messages they send and receive. What kind of relationships do they have with each other? Are they friends, family, coworkers, or strangers?

2. **Set the Tone with Opening Messages:**

   ○ Initialize the story with a set of messages or emails that establish the atmosphere. It could be a voicemail, a friendly chat, or a serious request.

3. **Develop the Plot Through Exchanges:**

   ○ Gradually build up the story through the digital conversations. Important details, conflict, and events that move the story forward are typically found in text messages and emails.

4. **Character Personalities in Writing Style:**

○ Your writing style should show what kind of person each character is. Think about the words they use, the emojis and words they use, and how official or casual their letters are written.

5. Progression of Time:

○ Use timestamps and dates in the texts and emails to show how time has passed. The pace or stress of a story can also be changed by the time between words.

6. Reveal Emotions and Reactions:

○ Show how you feel and what you're thinking through the words and tone of your texts. This can include joy, anger, confusion, or love.

7. Build Conflict and Resolution:

○ Introduce problems or disagreements into the digital conversation. These can be personal problems, misunderstandings, or pressures from outside sources. Build up to a conclusion or peak with such elements.

8. Use of Subject Lines and Signatures:

○ When you send emails, give hints about what the message is about or how it sounds in the subject line. Signatures can also add a personal touch or show what a character does for a living or how they act.

9. Conclusive Exchange:

○ Finish the story with a final set of emails or messages that wrap up the story, resolve the main conflicts, and reveal any last-minute surprises or twists.

CHAPTER 29

VOICE FROM THE PAST

Objective:

C REATE A MONOLOGUE THAT shows what a historical figure was thinking, feeling, and doing, giving us a glimpse into their life and times.

Guidelines:

1. Choose a Historical Figure:

- Figure out which historical figure's point of view you want to discover. Consider how important they were, what time period they lived in, and the events they were a part of.

2. Research and Context:

- Learn about the historical background, important events, and personal experiences of the person you've chosen by doing homework. This will build the monologue's credibility and depth.

3. Defining Moment or Reflection:

- Choose the time in the character's life from which the monologue will come. This could be a turning point, a crisis, a victory, or a time to think.

4. First-Person Perspective:

- Put yourself in the shoes of the historical figure and write in first person.

Their personality, the way they spoke, and the language of the time should all come through in the monologue.

5. Emotional Depth and Conflict:

○ Show how the character feels and what they are struggling with inside. How hard did things get for them? What did they hope for, fear, and want to do?

6. Expressing Ideals and Beliefs:

○ Describe with the person's beliefs, ideals, and contributions to their field or society. Do they think about what they did and the choices they made?

7. Interaction with Historical Events:

○ Talk about historical events or people who were important to them. How did these events change them or affect the way they saw things?

8. Personal Anecdotes and Experiences:

○ Add personal stories or experiences to make the character more real. This gives the historical story a more personal touch.

9. Concluding Thoughts:

○ Finish the monologue with a strong statement that sums up the person's legacy, accomplishments, or lessons learned.

CHAPTER 30

FULL CIRCLE

Objective:

W RITE A STORY THAT starts and ends with the same sentence. This will make the story go full circle, with the last repetition of the sentence taking on a whole new significance.

Guidelines:

1. **Crafting the Key Sentence:**

   ○ Start by writing an interesting, flexible sentence that can start or end your story. People should find this sentence interesting and be able to see it in different ways.

2. **Opening the Story:**

   ○ Put the chosen sentence at the beginning of your story. The sentence's first part should set the tone or mood or introduce a main character or theme.

3. **Developing the Plot:**

   ○ Create a story that follows the events described in the first sentence. The story should naturally move on from the first line's ideas or themes.

4. **Character and Conflict:**

   ○ Create your characters and their problems in a way that connects to the first sentence. How does what they go through and how they change during the story change the meaning towards that first line?

5. Progression and Change:

- ○ As the story goes on, add things (events, character growth, revelations) that make the reader rethink or reinterpret the first sentence.

6. Building to the Conclusion:

- ○ Lead the story to an end that naturally comes full circle back to the first sentence. The story should end with a resolution that makes the repeated sentence feel earned and meaningful.

7. Closing with the Same Sentence:

- ○ Use the same sentence from the beginning to end the story. However, the sentence should be understood in a different way now that the story has been told.

8. Reflecting on the Journey:

- ○ Repetition of the sentence should make the reader think about the journey and changes that have happened in the story, which should lead to a better or different understanding.

Chapter 31

TEMPEST ON THE CANVAS

Objective:

I MAGINE A PAINTING OF a stormy sea as the inspiration for a story. Your story should show the rough emotions, the raw power of nature, and the people who live in this setting.

Guidelines:

1. **Visual Description of the Painting**:

   ◦ First, talk about the painting. Pay close attention to the waves, colors, sky, and mood of the stormy sea. Is there a ship or people shown? How does the sea feel?

2. **Setting and Atmosphere**:

   ◦ Figure out what's going on in your story by looking at the painting. Giving your story the same intensity and mood as the painting, describe the setting in great detail.

3. **Character Introduction**:

   ◦ Include characters who are heading through or discovering the stormy sea. The painting's story should be connected to their past and why they are in this place.

4. **Emotional and Sensory Engagement**:

- Feel the emotions and use your senses to experience the scene. What do the characters feel when they see the stormy sea? Are they scared, amazed, excited, or hopeless?

5. Interplay of Nature and Characters:

- Figure out how the characters are connected to the sea. Is it a fight against nature, a sign of trouble inside, or a time to face the truth?

6. Conflict and Resolution:

- Build a conflict that the stormy setting leads to. How do the characters deal with this problem? What do they choose to do?

7. Reflecting the Painting's Themes:

- Bring the painting's ideas into your story, like how powerful nature is, how weak people are, or how beautiful chaos is.

8. Concluding the Scene:

- Finish the story in a way that connects to how you first described the painting. The ending should fit with the mood and themes of the painting.

9. Linking Art to Narrative:

- Don't lose sight of the painting as you write the story; let it shape the tone and direction of the story.

CHAPTER 32

MARKETPLACE MELODIES

Objective:

W RITE A STORY BASED on a picture of a busy, crowded market that shows the lively environment, the variety of people who are there, and the discussions that happen in this lively place.

Guidelines:

1. **Photograph Description:**

   ○ Start by describing the picture in full detail. Look at the busy market: the stands, the goods, the people, the colors, and the lively mood all around. What is the picture's most noticeable part?

2. **Setting and Atmosphere:**

   ○ You can use the photo's details to set the scene for your story. Describe the market's sounds, sights, and smells to make the scene realistic and authentic.

3. **Character Introduction:**

   ○ Add characters that are part of the market scene. They might be sellers, shoppers, or people just walking by. Make sure that each character has their own special characteristics and reason for being at the market.

4. **Interactions and Dynamics:**

- Create interactions between the characters that show how lively the market is. This could include negotiating prices, watching other people, having casual conversations, or running into someone you didn't expect to.

5. **Story Driven by Setting**:

- The setting in the market should drive the story. The story could be about a sale, a lost item, a chance meeting, or something that throws off the normal flow of the market.

6. **Cultural and Social Elements**:

- Add cultural and social details that give the market scene more depth. This could be about traditional goods, local customs, or the way people interact in the market.

7. **Conflict and Resolution**:

- Introduce in a problem or conflict that comes up in the crowded market. What do the characters do and say in response to this challenge?

8. **Concluding the Scene**:

- End up the story in a way that shows what the market is all about. This could be the end of the story's conflict, a character's realization, or a peaceful moment in the middle of all the action.

9. **Reflecting the Photograph's Essence**:

- Maintain a connection to the photo throughout the story, making sure that the story captures the spirit and atmosphere of the photo.

CHAPTER 33

ECHOES OF THE ABANDONED

Objective:

W RITE A STORY BASED on a picture of a mysterious empty house. Explore the mysteries it hides, the people who are drawn to it, and the old stories it whispers.

Guidelines:

1. **Description of the Image**:

   ○ Start by giving an extensive overview of the empty house in the picture. Look at how it looks on the outside, how old and neglected it looks, and how eerie it feels.

2. **Setting and Mood**:

   ○ The house should be the primary environment for your story. Describe the area around the house and how it fits with its mysterious sense. Set an atmosphere that fits the picture, whether it's scary, sad, or interesting.

3. **Introduction of Characters**:

   ○ Bring in characters who are attracted to or find the abandoned house by unintentionally. These could be people who live in the area, are interested in history, are urban explorers, or have a personal connection to the house.

4. Exploration and Discovery:

○ Tell what happens as the characters look around the house. What do they discover inside? Old photos, dusty furniture, and things having forgotten? Let each thing you find tell you something about the house's history or the story you want to tell.

5. Unraveling the House's History:

○ Gradually tell about the house's background. This could include information about the people who lived there before, important events that happened there, or why it ended up abandoned.

6. Character Connections to the House:

○ Find ways for the characters and the house to be connected. Do they have a family connection, a story that hasn't been told yet, or a fascination that comes from myths and tales?

7. Mystery or Conflict:

○ Add a main mystery or conflict which has something with the house. This could be something supernatural, a secret, or a personal quest that the characters need to complete.

8. Climactic Revelation:

○ Build up to a big reveal that lets you in on the house's secret. In this moment, you should feel deeply moved or learn something new.

9. Resolution and Aftermath:

○ Finish the story by figuring out the main mystery and showing what happened to the characters and the house afterward. What happens to the house? Does it get a new owner, or does it stay empty and hold its secrets?

CHAPTER 34

"IN THE GLOW OF DUSK"

Objective:

C REATE A STORY THAT captures the mood of a landscape at sunset, thinking about change, beauty, time passing, and reflection.

Guidelines:

1. **Describing the Sunset Landscape:**

- Start by describing thoroughly the landscape at sunset. Consider the sky's colors, how the light changes the scene, and how it makes you feel calm or reflective.

2. **Tone and Mood:**

- Make the story sound like a sunset. This could be a feeling of peace, sadness, hope, or the start and end of something.

3. **Character Introduction:**

- Add characters who are witnessing or being a part of this sunset scene. The way they feel and act should match the mood and themes of a sunset.

4. **Moments of Transition:**

- Come up with a story or character journeys that change like the day turns to night. Life changes, endings and beginnings, or moments of realizing and

5. Reflection and Contemplation:

- Use the story to get into the characters' thoughts or reflections. Like a sunset, these could be about remembering the past, pondering the present, or planning for the future.

6. Interactions and Relationships:

- Establish interactions between characters that are affected by the atmosphere of sunset. Intimate conversations, quiet company, or quiet reflection could be some of these.

7. Symbolism of the Sunset:

- Use sunset-related symbols, like the beauty of fleeting moments, the end of a phase, or the hope for what's to come after the dark.

8. Climactic Moment:

- Bring things to a climax or make a choice that fits with what the sunset means. This part of the story should be important to the character(s) and show what the story is about.

9. Resolution and Afterglow:

- End the story as the sun goes down and night comes. Think about what happened or what the characters learned, like how the afterglow of a sunset stays with you.

CHAPTER 35

THE PORTRAIT'S SECRET

Objective:

B ASED ON A PORTRAIT of a person with an interesting expression, write a detailed character description that goes into detail about their personality, background, and the story behind their expression.

Guidelines:

1. Detailed Description of the Expression:

- ○ First, give a detailed description of the person's face in the portrait. What's interesting about it? Is it mysterious, happy, sad, or defiant? Pay attention to the mouth, eyes, and other parts of the face that affect the expression.

2. Inferred Personality Traits:

- ○ Find out about the person's personality from the expression. Does the phrase imply intelligence, privacy, kindness, or maybe a troubled past? Use these hints to build the character's personality.

3. Physical Appearance:

- ○ Describe how the character looks based on what the portrait shows. Include information like your age, what you're wearing, how you stand, and any features that stand out, like hair color, scars, or jewelry.

4. Background and History:

○ Write the character's background story that explains their interesting expression. What kind of life experiences do they have? What are their social background, job, and important events in their life?

5. Current Situation or Conflict:

○ Think of a problem or situation the character is having right now that might explain their expression. It could be a problem inside them, a problem in their relationship, or a problem from their past.

6. Emotional and Psychological Depth:

○ Discover out more about the character's feelings and thoughts. What do they want, fear, and keep from you? How do these internal factors make their interesting expression possible?

7. Interactions with Others:

○ Think about how the character's face affects how they talk to other people. Do people get the wrong idea, or does it show more than the character wants to?

8. The Story Behind the Portrait:

○ Put an end to your portrait with a short story or scenario that sums up the character at that moment. They may be going through a big change or an important moment in their life.

CHAPTER 36

BEYOND THE SCULPTURE'S MOMENT

Objective:

W RITE A STORY ABOUT the events that happened before or after the scene shown in a famous sculpture. This will give the scene shown in the sculpture more meaning or a different point of view.

Guidelines:

1. **Choose a Famous Sculpture:**

   ○ Pick a famous sculpture that shows a unique scene or people. This could be a representation of something real, mythical, or abstract.

2. **Describing the Sculpture:**

   ○ Start by describing the sculpture in detail. Consider the figures' posture, facial expressions, movement, and the mood they create.

3. **Deciding the Timeframe:**

   ○ Whichever you choose, you can look at the events that happened before or right after the scene shown in the sculpture. This decision will affect how your story goes.

4. **Background and Context:**

○ Give information about the sculpture's scene's background or environment. Who are the people? In what stories or events from history do they appear?

5. Character Development:

○ Work on the sculpture's characters or figures. Give them feelings, thoughts, and personalities that go with the theme of the sculpture.

6. Building the Plot:

○ Develop a story that follows a logical path to or from the sculpture's moment, During the lead-up, you should create tension and excitement. Focusing on what happened after the event means showing the results or responses to it.

7. Emotional and Psychological Depth:

○ Learn more about how the characters are feeling and thinking. How do they feel about what's going on or where they are?

8. Climactic Moment or Consequences:

○ In the moments before the sculpture's moment, build up to a climax that flows smoothly into the scene. If it happens afterward, show what happened right away and how it changed the characters or the setting.

9. Conclusion and Reflection:

○ Bring the story full circle by linking it to the sculpture. Think about how your story gives the moment captured in the sculpture more meaning or depth.

CHAPTER 37

TOMORROW'S METROPOLIS

Objective:

IMAGINE A CITYSCAPE FROM the future and use it as inspiration for a story about the people, culture, and daily life in this advanced city.

Guidelines:

1. **Vivid Description of the Cityscape**:

   ○ Next, describe the picture of the cityscape from the future. Pay attention to the building, the technology, and the atmosphere in general. Are there tall skyscrapers, flying cars, and high-tech buildings?

2. **Setting and World-Building**:

   ○ You can use the picture's details to set the scene for your story. How does this city from the future work? How have technologies changed and what are the rules of society?

3. **Introduction of Characters**:

   ○ Introduce to individuals who live or work in this cityscape. Give them different pasts and roles that make sense in a futuristic world. How do they interact with the world around them?

4. Daily Life and Technology:

- Find out what the characters do every day in this high-tech city. What changes about their daily lives, relationships, and problems because of technology?

5. Cultural and Social Elements:

- Culture and society from the future should have their own unique parts. New ways to have fun, talk to each other, or organize social groups could be part of this.

6. Plot Driven by the Setting:

- Create a story that is deeply connected to the futuristic parts of the city. This could be about a new piece of technology, a problem in society, or a personal quest in the city.

7. Conflict and Resolution:

- Bring in a problem or conflict that has to do with living in the futuristic city. How do the characters get through this and solve the problem?

8. Themes and Messages:

- Include ideas like how technology has changed society, the difficulties of living in cities in the future, or what it's like to be human in a world full of new technologies.

9. Concluding Reflection:

- At the end of the story, think about the characters' journeys and what makes the city unique. What messages or insights does the story send about the future?

CHAPTER 38

ECHOES OF THE ABSTRACT

Objective:

W RITE A STORY BASED on the feelings, colors, shapes, and overall mood of an abstract art piece. Use the non-representational parts to make the story flow and be creative.

Guidelines:

1. **Interpreting the Abstract Art Piece**:

   ○ Start by figuring out what the abstract art piece means. Name the shades, shapes, lines, and textures. In what ways or ways does the piece make you feel? Is it crazy, calm, passionate, or mysterious?

2. **Setting and Atmosphere**:

   ○ Establish the tone and mood of your story by using the art piece's mood. If the art is bright and disorganized, the story may take place in a world that is fast-paced and chaotic. The atmosphere could be calm or reflective if it's simple and calm.

3. **Character Creation**:

   ○ Make characters whose feelings and experiences are like the art piece. The themes and feelings you got from the art should connect with their personalities, problems, and journeys.

4. Plot Inspired by Art:

○ Think of a plot that goes with the abstract style of the art. This could include stories that don't follow a straight line, events that are symbolic, or experiences that are like the visual parts of the art.

5. Emotional and Psychological Depth:

○ In a way that looks like the art, look into the emotional and mental parts of your characters. How do they see the world around them and interact with it? What disagreements do they have with each other?

6. Incorporating Abstract Elements:

○ Adding abstract ideas to the story is important. This could mean messing with reality, using strange or symbolic situations, or telling the story in a way that isn't typical.

7. Climactic Moment or Revelation:

○ Build up to an emotional or thematic climax or revelation that fits with how you first understood the art.

8. Resolution and Interpretation:

○ Finish the story in a way that makes you think of the abstract art piece again. Like the art itself, the ending should fit with the first interpretation while also leaving room for other ones.

9. Reflecting the Artistic Essence:

○ Keep the story connected to the abstract art's essence, making sure that the story captures the piece's spirit and emotional impact.

CHAPTER 39

LEGEND OF THE MYTHICAL BEAST

Objective:

M AKE UP A FANTASY story about a creature from a myth that is shown in a picture. The story should explore where the creature came from, how it interacts with the world, and the myths that surround it.

Guidelines:

1. **Description of the Mythical Creature:**

    ◦ Start by describing the creature from the myth that is shown in the picture. Pay attention to its appearance, behavior, and any unique traits that make it stand out.

2. **World-Building:**

    ◦ Set up the fantasy world where the monster lives. Describe the world's landscape, its people, and how mythical creatures are seen there. Does the creature show up often or not often?

3. **Creature's Origins and Mythos:**

    ◦ Make up a story or myth about the creature. How did the thing come to be? In the fantasy world, are there myths or stories about it?

4. Main Characters and Their Encounter:

- Describe the main people in your story. How do they find the mythical creature and talk to it? Who are they? Are they explorers, locals, or creatures from mythology?

5. Creature's Impact on the World:

- Find out what the creature does to the world around it. Does it bring luck, fear, or awe? What do people do when it's around?

6. Adventure or Conflict:

- Think up with a story that involves the creature. It could be an adventure to find it, a conflict caused by what it does, or a quest related to the fact that it exists.

7. Themes and Symbolism:

- Include ideas or symbols that are connected to the creature. Subjects could be nature, power, mystery, or something unknown.

8. Climactic Interaction:

- The creature should be the focus of a building-up scene. A dramatic revelation, an important conversation with a character, or a turning point that changes everything could be this.

9. Resolution and Legend Continues:

- Finish the story by figuring out what happened with the main plot. Think about how meeting the creature has changed the characters or the world. Does the creature's story get bigger, or does it fade back into myth?

CHAPTER 40

NOIR SHADOWS

Objective:

C REATE A MYSTERY STORY based on the mood and imagery of a noir-style photograph of a city at night. The story should include elements of suspense, intrigue, and the dark atmosphere of the city.

Guidelines:

1. **Noir Atmosphere Description:**

   ○ Describe the atmosphere that the noir-style photo shows to start with. Pay attention to the way the light and shadows move, the buildings that are only partially visible, the streets that are empty or full of people, and the overall feeling of danger and mystery.

2. **Setting the Scene:**

   ○ Figure out where your story takes place in a way that fits the noir style. Explain how the city at night changes into a character in your mystery by talking about its sounds, sights, and smells.

3. **Introduction of Main Character:**

   ○ Make your main character, who should be in the noir genre, known. This could be a detective, a witness, someone with a strange past, or someone who got caught up in something out of the blue.

4. Inciting Incident:

○ Show the event or mystery that the story is about. This could be a crime, a missing person, a strange message, or a strange encounter.

5. Investigation and Clues:

○ Watch as the character looks into what happens. What do they do to find clues? How do they interact with other characters? What problems do they face in the dark, noir city?

6. Suspense and Danger:

○ Add some suspense and danger to the story. With its dark corners, unknown dangers, and characters' inner struggles, the noir setting should make things more tense.

7. Plot Twists and Red Herrings:

○ To keep the reader guessing, use plot twists and red herrings. Because noir stories are usually complicated, the answer to the mystery shouldn't be easy to find.

8. Climactic Revelation:

○ Eventually lead to a big reveal or fight where the mystery is solved. Based on what the story has shown, this should be both surprising and satisfying.

9. Resolution and Reflection:

○ Complete the story by solving the mystery and thinking about what it all means. What effect does the resolution have on the character and how they see the city?

CHAPTER 41

A RENEWED WORLD

Objective:

W RITE A STORY THAT takes place in the future, after people have stopped climate change and looked into the changes that happened in society, technology, and the environment that made this possible.

Guidelines:

1. **Environmental Transformation:**

   ○ Start by writing about how the world is now that climate change has stopped. What does the setting look like? In what ways have ecosystems and animals grown back?

2. **Technological and Societal Changes:**

   ○ Give examples of the new technologies and changes in society that helped stop climate change. Think about big steps forward in renewable energy, changes in economic and political priorities, and working together around the world.

3. **Character Perspectives:**

   ○ Introduce characters who have seen these changes happen or have helped make them happen. Their points of view can give the global change a more personal touch.

4. **Life in the Renewed World**:

  ○ Find out what life is like in this world every day. In this new era, how do people, communities, and governments work differently?

5. **Reflections on the Past**:

  ○ Think about or remember the time when climate change was a very serious threat. What do the characters think about those times compared to now?

6. **Challenges and Adaptations**:

  ○ Still, think about what new problems or ways of doing things society has to deal with now that the good changes have happened. Since climate change has been stopped, what are the new issues or priorities?

7. **Cultural and Global Shifts**:

  ○ Explain the changes in culture that have taken place. How have people's views on the environment, consumption, and long-term living changed?

8. **Individual and Collective Journeys**:

  ○ Take a glimpse at the paths that people and groups took to accomplish this change. One example of this would be protesting, making progress in science, or changing the rules.

9. **Conclusion and Future Outlook**:

  ○ At the end of the story, think about what will happen next. What have we learned, and how can we use it to make sure the future is sustainable?

CHAPTER 42

YOUTHFUL REVOLUTION

Objective:

W RITE A STORY ABOUT a teenager who starts a movement to address a major social issue. The story should show the teen's journey as an activist, the problems they face, and the change they bring about.

Guidelines:

1. **Character Introduction:**

   ○ Describe the main protagonist as a teen. Include information about their background, personality, and the reason they want to do something about a certain social issue.

2. **Social Issue Identification:**

   ○ Make it clear what social issue the teen cares deeply about. What does it mean for them, their community, and society as a whole?

3. **The Spark for Action:**

   ○ Describe the event that makes the teen want to start a movement. This could be a personal experience, something they saw happen, or a realization of how important the issue is.

4. **Formation of the Movement:**

- Show the primary steps that were taken to begin the movement. This could mean getting support from friends and family, using social media to raise awareness, or planning the first event or protest.

5. **Challenges and Obstacles**:

- Describe the problems the teen has building and maintaining the movement. These could be questions from adults, opposition, problems with getting things done, or disagreements within the movement.

6. **Growth and Impact**:

- Look into how the movement gets bigger and starts to influence. What does society or the community do? What kinds of changes or conversations are started?

7. **Personal Development**:

- Show how the teen's growth is affected by leading the movement. How do they learn to be leaders, be strong, and be activists?

8. **Climactic Event**:

- Build up to a big event that will test the movement's resolve or show them where they need to go next.

9. **Resolution and Reflection**:

- At the end of the story, show what happened with the movement. Think about the changes the movement has made and where it might go from here.

10. **Themes and Messages**:

- Use ideas like social responsibility, the power of youth activism, and how important it is to stand up for what's right.

CHAPTER 43

HEART OF THE COMMUNITY

Objective:

W RITE A STORY ABOUT someone who plans an event for their community to support a good cause. Focus on their reasons, the problems they face, and the results of their work.

Guidelines:

1. **Character Introduction:**

   ○ Start off by introducing your main character. Why do they want to put together this event? How do they feel about or have a connection to the cause?

2. **Choosing the Cause:**

   ○ Describe the good cause that the event is being held for. Why is it significant to the person and the neighborhood?

3. **Planning the Event:**

   ○ Explain the early steps of making plans for the event. What kind of event is it (a benefit, a campaign to raise awareness, or volunteer work)? In what way does the character start to carry out their plan?

4. Gathering Support:

- ○ In your writing, show how the character asks for and gets help from others. Some ways to do this are to ask for donations, get people to volunteer, or involve local businesses.

5. Overcoming Obstacles:

- ○ Summarize the problems and challenges the character faces as they try to plan the event. These could be problems with logistics, a lack of resources, or doubts from other people.

6. Personal Growth and Relationships:

- ○ Find out how the character's personal growth is affected by the process of planning the event. What changes in their relationships with other people in the community?

7. The Event Unfolds:

- ○ Consider speaking about the event day. Write down the mood, the number of people who showed up, and the activities that were going on. Seeing their hard work pay off: how does the character feel?

8. Impact and Reflection:

- ○ Show how the event helped the cause and the neighborhood. How does the character's attitude change after the event or its outcome?

9. Concluding Thoughts:

- ○ Finish the story with the character thinking about their journey. In what ways did they learn? What effects did planning the event for a good cause have on them and their neighborhood?

CHAPTER 44

RIPPLES OF CHANGE

Objective:

S TAND UP WITH A story about a character whose life, beliefs, and actions are all changed by a major current event.

Guidelines:

1. **Selection of Current Event**:

   ○ Pick a big event happening right now to use as a backdrop for your story. This could be a health crisis, a natural disaster, a political movement, or a big step forward in technology.

2. **Character Introduction**:

   ○ Describe your main character. Give some background on their life before the event. How is their current situation or way of thinking different from how it was before the event?

3. **Event Impact**:

   ○ Explain us how the current event affects the character, either directly or indirectly. This could be a loss of a loved one, a change in circumstances, or a change in how you see the world.

4. **Emotional and Psychological Response**:

- Figure out how the character felt and thought about what happened. How do they deal with the risks or changes that come with it?

5. Altered Life Trajectory:

- Show how the event changes the character's future. What do they do? Do they get involved in activism, change careers, or move? What changes about their goals and relationships?

6. Challenges and Adaptation:

- Make the character face problems because of what happened. How do they deal with these problems or adjust to new situations?

7. Character Development:

- Show how the character changes as the story goes on. How does what they've learned about the current event help them grow as a person or change the way they see things?

8. Climactic Moment:

- Bring the story to a climax that has something to do with how the character is feeling about what's happening. It could be something they do, a choice they make, or an insight they have.

9. Resolution and Reflection:

- End the story by showing how the character combines what they've learned with their new life. Thoughtfully consider how the current event affects their life and community as a whole.

10. Themes and Messages:

- Implement ideas like adaptability, change, social responsibility, and how world events affect people's lives.

CHAPTER 45

CLASH OF PERSPECTIVES

Objective:

W RITE AN INTERESTING AND detailed conversation between two characters who have different opinions on a social issue. Show their arguments, feelings, and how complicated the topic is.

Guidelines:

1. **Choosing the Social Topic:**

   ○ Pick a social issue that is relevant and can be debated. This could be about climate change, equal rights for everyone, changing the way schools work, or how technology changes society.

2. **Character Creation:**

   ○ Create two characters who have different backgrounds and views on the subject you chose. Their experiences, values, and beliefs should shape what they think.

3. **Opening the Dialogue:**

   ○ Initiate the conversation in a way that makes the subject come up on its own. It could be a direct argument, a news story that starts a conversation, or an event that both of them are interested in.

4. **Presenting Arguments:**

○ Give each character a chance to make their side of the story. They should be able to clearly explain their points of view with logic, emotional appeals, or personal stories.

5. Emotional Responses and Tension:

○ Stress and emotional responses should be included. The characters' words should show how strongly they feel about their position.

6. Listening and Responding:

○ The dialogue should show how strongly and passionately each character feels about their role.

7. Exploring Complexity:

○ Use the conversation to get to the bottom of how complicated and deep the subject is. Talk about common misunderstandings, moral problems, and what each point of view means for society as entirety.

8. Avoiding Resolution:

○ The conversation doesn't have to end the argument. It's often more realistic and makes you think if each character stays true to what they believe, even if they learn more about the other side.

9. Concluding the Dialogue:

○ At the end of the conversation, sum up what was said with a statement, a thought-provoking question, or a moment of silence.

CHAPTER 46

TECH FOR THE EARTH

Objective:

W RITE A STORY ABOUT a character who uses new technology to solve an environmental problem in their area. Show the difficulties, the steps they take, and the results of their actions.

Guidelines:

1. Environmental Issue Introduction:

- ○ Get started by talking about the local environmental issue. There might be pollution, deforestation, a lack of water, or animals in the character's community that are in danger.

2. Character Background:

- ○ Describe your main character. Tell us about their background, especially how they are connected to technology and the environment. Why do they want to solve this problem so badly?

3. Technological Solution Concept:

- ○ Explain the technology that the character comes up with or suggests as a way to help the environment. Simply describe how it works. What makes it a good solution for this problem?

4. Development and Challenges:

○ Show the steps that were taken to create and use the technology. Include the problems the character is having, like technical issues, lack of money, or doubts from the community.

5. Testing and Application:

○ Describe the testing and use phases of the technology solution. How does the character make sure that it works and is safe?

6. Community Involvement:

○ Find out what the character does to help the community or use the technology. How does the neighborhood feel? Are there changes in how people feel or act about the environment?

7. Impact on the Environment:

○ What effect does the technology have on the problem with the environment? What good things start to happen? How is the local ecosystem's balance fixed or made better?

8. Personal Growth and Reflection:

○ Think about how the character has changed over the course of the story. How has using technology to deal with environmental problems changed them?

9. Conclusion and Future Implications:

○ Finally, think about what the success of the technology means for society entirety. What does this mean for environmental problems that might come up in the community or elsewhere?

CHAPTER 47

A DAY OF CHANGE

Objective:

W RITE A STORY ABOUT a teenage activist who fights hard for a cause every day, showing what they do, the problems they face, and what drives them.

Guidelines:

1. **Introduction of the Teen Activist:**

   ○ Bring up the teen activist to get started. Give information about their background, the cause they're fighting for, and what drives them to be an activist.

2. **Starting the Day:**

   ○ How does their day start? In connection with their activism, what habits or preparations do they make? Some of the things that could be done are planning, researching, or getting in touch with other activists.

3. **School Life and Activism:**

   ○ Show how their work as an activist affects their time as a student. What do they do to balance their activism with their schoolwork? Are they a part of any school-based programs?

4. **Engagement in Activism Activities:**

   ○ Describe those particular things they do during the day. For example, they might go to or plan protests, meetings, social media campaigns, or community events.

5. Challenges Faced:

  ○ Mention the problems they face as a teen activist. These problems could include opposition, trouble managing their time, or discovering effective ways to be heard.

6. Interactions with Peers and Community:

  ○ Find out how they interact with family, friends, and people in the community. How do the people around them feel about their beliefs and activism?

7. Key Event or Action:

  ○ As part of their day, include an important event that marks a turning point in their activism. This could be a new start, a setback, a chance to learn, or a time when someone helps you.

8. Personal Reflection and Growth:

  ○ Have times when the character thinks about their journey, how their activism has affected others, and what they want to do in the future. What do they think their part is in the cause they're going after?

9. Evening Routine and Looking Forward:

  ○ Finally, write about how they end their day. This could mean making plans for future activist activities, thinking about the day's successes and failures, or getting in touch with people who support them.

10. Themes and Messages:

  ○ Include ideas like how important it is to stand up for what you believe in, how powerful it is for young people to speak out, and how resilient people can be.

CHAPTER 48

UNITY IN ADVERSITY

Objective:

W RITE A STORY ABOUT how people in a community come together to help a beloved local business that is having a hard time. The story should show the spirit of community, solidarity, and resilience.

Guidelines:

1. **Introduction of the Local Business:**

   ○ Start by telling them about the local business. Explain what it does for the community, how it came to be, and why people love it. What types of problems does the company have?

2. **Business Owner's Struggle:**

   ○ Introduce the business owner. Give some information about how hard it is for them to keep the business going. Why are they having trouble? How do they feel about the idea of closing?

3. **Community's Initial Reaction:**

   ○ Show how people in the area react when they hear that the business is having problems. Feel what they're feeling: loss, worry, and the desire to help.

4. **Organizing Support:**

- Describe the steps that people in the community took to get help. This could include things like social media campaigns, fundraising events, or volunteer work.

5. **Diverse Community Involvement**:

- Bring attention to the different people in the community who are involved. In your own words, describe how each person and each group makes a difference.

6. **Challenges in the Effort**:

- Talk about the problems the community is having when they try to help the business. How are they going to get past these problems?

7. **Personal Stories and Connections**:

- Include personal stories of people in the community who have something to do with the business. What changes their lives because of the business?

8. **Climactic Event**:

- Get ready for a big event or moment that will show how much the community cares. It's possible that this will be a big turning point for the business.

9. **Resolution and Impact**:

- At the end of the story, show what happened because of the community's activity. Think about how their willingness to work together affected the business and the community's sense of unity.

10. **Themes and Reflection**:

- Include ideas about community, strength, and how important it is to buy from local businesses. Think about what the community and the business owner have learned from this.

Chapter 49

CONNECTIONS IN A
DIGITAL AGE

Objective:

W RITE A STORY THAT shows how social media affects the relationships between the characters, pointing out both the good and bad things about using technology.

Guidelines:

1. **Character Introduction**:

   ○ Start by introducing your main characters. Create unique characters with backgrounds and personalities, and explain how they use social media. They could be active users, skeptics, influencers, or passive observers.

2. **Relationship Dynamics**:

   ○ Determine how your characters are connected to each other. This could include family ties, friendships, romantic relationships, or connections at work. How does social media affect these relationships at first?

3. **Social Media as a Catalyst**:

   ○ Use social media to set off the events of the story. This could be a misunderstanding caused by talking or posting something online, a connection made or lost on social media, or how a character feels about something they see online.

4. Contrasting Perspectives:

o Give different points of view on how social media affects relationships. Show how the online interactions of different characters affect them and how they are affected by them.

5. Challenges and Conflicts:

o Talk about problems or issues that come up when you use social media. This could include privacy issues, misunderstandings, the difference between an online persona and the real persona, or how digital connections affect relationships in real life.

6. Development and Resolution:

o Show how the characters deal with the problems that social media brings up to move the story forward. How do they work out their differences, and what changes in their relationships as a result?

7. Positive and Negative Impact:

o Examine both the good and bad effects of social media. What does it do to bring people together or separate them? How does it change the way they talk to each other and understand each other?

8. Character Growth:

o Utilize their experiences with social media to display how they have grown as people. Do they learn how to balance talking to people in person with talking to people online? How does their view of social media change over time?

9. Conclusion and Reflection:

o In the end of the story, think about what you've learned about how social media affects relationships. What do the characters and the story as a whole say about how people connect with technology these days?

CHAPTER 50

A MOSAIC OF CULTURES

Objective:

WRITE A STORY ABOUT a character's interactions and experiences with people from different cultures at school or in their neighborhood. Show the difficulties, teaching moments, and beauty of multicultural settings.

Guidelines:

1. Character Introduction:

○ Start by introducing your main character. Include information about their past and how they first felt about cultural diversity. Or have they been a part of a diverse environment their whole lives?

2. Diverse Setting Description:

○ Describe the school or neighborhood. What makes it different in terms of culture? Show off the different languages, traditions, cuisines, and ways of life that can be found in the area.

3. Initial Encounters and Challenges:

○ Explain the character's first experiences with people from other cultures. Such problems can be misunderstandings, language barriers, or traditions and customs that are not familiar.

4. Learning and Adaptation:

- Show how the character learns about and adjusts to different cultures. How do they get past the problems they face at first? What kinds of experiences help them see things from different points of view?

5. Interactions with Peers:

- Observe how the character interacts with their peers who come from different backgrounds. What changes in their understanding and appreciation of other cultures because of these interactions?

6. Moments of Appreciation and Connection:

- There should be times when the character understands and appreciates other cultures. This could be done through festivals, activities that everyone does together, food, music, or stories.

7. Addressing Prejudices and Stereotypes:

- Show how the character faces and gets past any biases or stereotypes if it's important. How do these new facts change their view?

8. Cultural Celebration Event:

- A cultural celebration or event could be the story's climax. This is where the character fully experiences and participates in the diverse community.

9. Character Growth and Reflection:

- Think about how the character changes as they go through life. What do they know now about different cultures, getting along with others, and sticking together?

10. Conclusion and Future Outlook:

- Finally, talk about how the character feels about living in a place with a lot of different cultures. What do they think about their place in this mix of cultures?

CHAPTER 51

ASPIRING TO MY DREAM JOB

Objective:

W RITE A PERSONAL REFLECTION about your dream job and the steps you plan to take to get it. Include what motivates you, what challenges you face, and what your goals are along the way.

Guidelines:

1. **Dream Job Description:**

   ○ Define your dream job in detail to begin. Describe the type of work. What draws you to it? Does this job fit with your skills, values, and interests?

2. **Initial Inspiration:**

   ○ Consider what made you want to pursue this dream job. Was there a turning point, a person who influenced you, or a slow but steady realization of your goals and interests?

3. **Skills and Qualifications Needed:**

   ○ Find out what skills and accomplishments will be required for the job you want. What kind of schooling, training, or work experience do you need?

4. **Steps Towards the Dream Job:**

○ Explain the steps you're going to take or have already taken to get your dream job. This could include your schooling, internships, ways of making connections, or other activities that are relevant.

5. Challenges and Obstacles:

○ Understand and accept any problems or challenges you may face on your journey. How are you going to deal with these problems?

6. Personal Growth and Development:

ı Talk about how going after your dream job helps you grow as a person. What do you want to learn or have you learned along the way?

7. Support and Influence:

○ Analyze how others have helped and influenced you on your journey. What role have mentors, family, friends, or peers played in your goal?

8. Future Vision and Goals:

○ Explain what you want to do with your life after you get your dream job. What are your goals for your career and personal growth in that job?

9. Reflection on Impact:

○ Make a list about how you want to make a difference at your dream job. In what ways do you want to make a difference in your community, the world, or your field?

10. Concluding Thoughts:

○ Finish by thinking about how important it is to go after your dream job. What does this trip mean to you, and what do you want to say to people who want to do the same thing?

CHAPTER 52

OVERCOMING AND LEARNING

Objective:

W RITE A FICTIONAL STORY about a difficult event that happened to you, how you handled it, and the important lessons you learned from it.

Guidelines:

1. **Introduction of the Challenge**:

   ○ Start by talking about the problem you had. Describe the situation and explain why it was hard for you. This will set the scene.

2. **Initial Reactions and Feelings**:

   ○ Think about how you felt and what you did when you first faced the challenge. Were you worried, determined, or stressed out?

3. **Approach and Actions Taken**:

   ○ Describe the steps you took to deal with or get past the problem. Did you ask for help, make a plan, or learn something new? How did you keep going when you were having doubts or problems?

4. **Obstacles and Setbacks**:

○ Talk about any problems or setbacks you ran into along the way. How did these problems test your strength of will, and how did you deal with them?

5. Support and Resources:

○ Recognize the help and resources that got you through the challenge. Persons like friends, family, mentors, or personal research could be included.

6. Resolution of the Challenge:

○ Describe how the problem was finally solved. What happened? How did you feel when you got through the tough part?

7. Lessons Learned:

○ Think about what you learned from facing the challenge and getting through it. How did the event change the way you think about or solve problems?

8. Personal Growth and Development:

○ Focus of what the challenge did to help you grow as a person. What strengths did you learn or grow? How has the event changed the way you make decisions or act in the future?

9. Advice and Insights:

○ Give advice or your thoughts based on what you know. What would you tell someone who is going through the same thing?

10. Concluding Thoughts:

○ Finish by thinking about how important it is to face challenges. What do you think about problems now, and how has this experience helped you get ready for future problems?

CHAPTER 53

DIALOGUE ACROSS TIME

Objective:

W RITE A CONVERSATION BETWEEN your present self and your future self. Pay attention to the questions, suggestions, and new ideas that come up during this conversation.

Guidelines:

1. **Setting the Scene**:

   ○ Start by making the conversation's situation clear. How do you meet your future self? Is it a dream, a technological marvel, or just a thought?

2. **Characterization of Both Selves**:

   ○ Determine both the person you are now and the person you will be in the future. How does your future self look, act, or see things differently?

3. **Initial Questions and Reactions**:

   ○ Start the conversation by saying what you think and asking questions. What do you want to know first from yourself in the future?

4. **Life Updates and Changes**:

   ○ Share with your future self what's going on in your life. What big changes or important events have happened? This could include things like family, career, or lifestyle changes, as well as personal accomplishments.

5. Advice from the Future:

o Allow your future self to give you advice. What do they teach you or warn you about? In this case, it could be about specific problems, big choices in life, or staying healthy and happy.

6. Reflections on Past Decisions:

o Think about how decisions have turned out in the past. In what ways does your future self see the decisions you made in the past? Do you have any regrets or moments of pride?

7. Questions about the World:

o Think about what the world will be like in the future. What changes have happened in society, in technology, or around the world?

8. Personal Growth and Lessons:

o Think about themes like growing as a person and lessons learned over time. How has the way your future self thinks and acts changed over time?

9. Closing Message and Wisdom:

o Finish the conversation with a wise or meaningful message from yourself in the future. What are their last thoughts?

10. Reflection on the Conversation:

o Finally, end by thinking about the conversation as you are now. What changes do you think it has made in your current life choices and how you think about the future?

CHAPTER 54

ECHOES OF A CHERISHED MEMORY

Objective:

W RITE A NARRATIVE ABOUT a memorable event that you hold precious. Include details about how you felt at the time, what happened, and how it has affected or changed your life since then.

Guidelines:

1. **Describing the Memory**:

   ○ Begin by describing the special memory in excessive detail. Tell the reader where it happened, who was there, and what happened to set the scene. Add details about the senses to make the memory come alive.

2. **Emotional Landscape**:

   ○ Think about how you felt when you remembered the event. Were you pleased, thrilled, calm, or amazed? Explain what made you feel these ways.

3. **Significance of the Moment**:

   ○ Define why this memory is important and dear to you. In what ways did it change your life, connect you with someone special, or teach you a valuable lesson?

4. Personal Connections:

○ Talk about the personal ties that this memory has to you. Are there certain people who made it unique? How did this event add to or take away from your relationships?

5. Reflection on Changes Over Time:

○ Think about how your memories of this event have changed over time. Has it become more important? Do the events seem different to you now that you're older or have more life experience?

6. Impact on Your Life:

○ Think about how this memory has changed your life over time. How has it changed your mind, choices, or values? Has it changed your interests, job, or relationships?

7. Nostalgia and Learning:

○ Think about how this memory makes you feel nostalgic. What do you recall about it now? How does it continue to make you feel good or inspire you?

8. Comparing Past and Present:

○ Look at how your life was different or the same when you remember something. Since then, how have you grown or changed?

9. Concluding Thoughts:

○ Last but not least, think about how important it is to hold on to memories. What does this memory tell you about the future?

CHAPTER 55

A MOMENT OF PRIDE

Objective:

W RITE ABOUT AN INCIDENT when you were really proud of yourself. Include specifics about the situation, what you did, and why this moment was important to you.

Guidelines:

1. **Describing the Proud Moment:**

   ◦ Start by imagining the time you were proud. What happened in that case? Was it about a personal goal, a challenge, a good deed, or a success?

2. **Lead-Up to the Moment:**

   ◦ Describe the stages or events that led up to this point. What were some of the problems you had? What kind of hard work or planning went into it?

3. **The Achieving Act:**

   ◦ Describe a specific thing you did or accomplished that made you proud. Did you finish a project, stand up for what you believe in, help someone, or get over a fear?

4. **Emotional Response:**

   ◦ Simply think about how you felt at that time. How did it feel to know that you had done something great? What kind of happiness, fulfillment, or satisfaction did you feel?

5. Personal Significance:

- Explain what made this event so important to you. Did it mark an important event, help you grow as a person, or prove your skills or beliefs?

6. Overcoming Obstacles:

- Discuss any problems or self-doubts you overcame, if applicable. How did overcoming these problems make you feel proud?

7. Learning and Growth:

- Think about what this experience taught you about yourself. How did this proud moment help you grow as a person or change how you see yourself?

8. Impact on Future Actions:

- Discuss about how this moment of pride has affected what you've done or decided since then. Has it made you want to set new goals or changed how you'll deal with problems in the future?

9. Concluding Reflection:

- Finally, think about how important it is to recognize and celebrate your successes. What message or piece of advice would you give to people who want to find pride in their own lives?

CHAPTER 56

THE GIFT OF GIVING

Objective:

I F YOU HELPED SOMEONE, write something about it that focuses on the situation, what you did, how it affected the person you helped, and how you felt.

Guidelines:

1. **Context of the Helping Situation:**

   ○ Start by describing the context. Describe the situation where you could have helped someone. Who were you helping? What did they need or have a problem with?

2. **Your Decision to Help:**

   ○ Define what made you want to help. Was it a natural reaction, a sense of duty, or something your own values or past experiences pushed you to do?

3. **Describing the Act of Helping:**

   ○ Describe the things you did to help. This could be anything from a small act of kindness to a big one of support or sacrifice.

4. **The Recipient's Response:**

   ○ Memrize how the person you helped responded. How did they react when you helped them? How did your help change their situation or feelings right away?

5. Your Emotional Response:

- Consider how you felt while you were helping others and afterward. At that moment, did you feel happy, fulfilled, compassionate, or maybe even stuck?

6. Reflections on the Impact:

- When you do something, think about how it will affect other people. How did helping this person change the way you think about other people's problems or needs? Did it change how you feel about helping people?

7. Personal Learning and Growth:

- Take note about what you learned from this event. In what ways did it help you grow as a person? Did it make your values or beliefs stronger?

8. The Importance of Helping Others:

- Summarize what you believe about how important it is to help other people. What part of being kind and helpful in a community did this experience teach or reinforce for you?

9. Concluding Thoughts:

- Finally, give a brief summary of how helping someone made you feel and how important you think acts of kindness and compassion are.

CHAPTER 57

MY LIFE ON SCREEN

Objective:

MAKE A PLOT SCRIPT for a movie about your life, focusing on the most important scenes that show important events, turning points, and emotional journeys.

Guidelines:

1. **Opening Scene (Background and Introduction):**

   ○ Place your life story in its proper context with an opening scene. Your childhood, your family history, or a big event in your early life that shapes who you are could be this.

2. **Key Childhood Moment:**

   ○ Include a scene from your childhood that you will always remember. This could be a special moment with your family, a challenge you faced as a child, or an event that sparked an interest that will last a lifetime.

3. **Defining Teenage Experience:**

   ○ Write about a moment from your teen years that helped shape who you are now. This could include things like school, friendships, first loves, or fights that changed your path.

4. **Major Life Decision:**

○ Draw a scene where you make a big choice in your life. This could mean picking a career path, moving to a new area, or following a passion.

5. Triumph and Challenge:

○ Write a scene that shows an important victory or challenge in your life. This could be a big moment in your life, a professional accomplishment, or a personal struggle.

6. Moment of Self-Discovery:

○ Include a time when you learned something about yourself. This scene should show a turning point in your life where you learn something impor tant about yourself or the path you want to take in life.

7. Relationships and Connections:

○ You should add scenarios that are about relationships that are important to you. If you have any, they should be with family, friends, or significant others and show how they have affected you.

8. Current Life Snapshot:

○ Show how your life is right now by making a scene. What are you doing every day, what are your problems and what are your joys? How do the things that happened to you in the past affect the way you live now?

9. Imagining the Future (Climactic Scene):

○ A dramatic scene will take place in the future. You could use a scene that shows what you want to do or become, a dream coming true, or something you imagine yourself achieving in the future.

10. Reflective Closing Scene:

○ Finish with a scene that makes you think about your life and how it all fits together. You could be talking to yourself, having a conversation with someone important to you, or just taking some time to think.

11. **Narrative Themes**:

- In the movie outline, you should draw attention to themes like change, strength, following your dreams, and how important relationships are.

CHAPTER 58

1NFLUENCER OF MY PATH

Objective:

WRITE A PIECE OF thought about someone who has had a big impact on your life. Focus on their effect, the lessons they've taught you, and how they've made you who you are.

Guidelines:

1. **Introduction of the Influential Person**:

   ○ Start by introducing the person who has helped you. Explain what relationship you have with them and how you met them in the first place.

2. **Character Traits and Qualities**:

   ○ Write down the things about this person's character that you admire and find significant. What about their personality, actions, or way of life has affected you?

3. **Specific Instances of Influence**:

   ○ Think back to specific times or events when this person had a big impact on your life. This could be through what they do, say, give, or support.

4. **Lessons Learned**:

   ○ Discuss about the specific lessons or values they taught you. How have these lessons changed the way you make choices, act, or think about life?

5. Changes in Your Life:

○ Make a list about how this person has made your life different or better. Think about the ways that their influence has changed your attitude, goals, or life path.

6. Challenges and Support:

○ If applicable, talk about times when this person helped you get through tough times. What difference did their help or advice make when things were hard?

7. Their Own Challenges and Strengths:

○ Think about their own problems and strengths. How have their stories and ability to keep going inspired you or given you a model to follow?

8. Emotional Connection:

○ Discover about the way you feel about this person. How do they make you feel? Are you impressed, thankful, or inspired?

9. Continued Influence:

○ Think about how their influence on your life is still recognized. In what ways do you use their lessons, values, or ideas in your current life?

10. Concluding Thoughts:

○ Finally, give a brief summary of how they affected you overall. What tribute or message do you want to send about how they've changed your life?

CHAPTER 59

JOURNEY TOWARDS MY GOAL

Objective:

W RITE AN ANALYSIS ABOUT a personal goal you have set for yourself. In it, describe the steps you are taking to reach your goal, the problems you are facing, and what drives you to do so.

Guidelines:

1. **Goal Description:**

   ○ Start by giving a clear description of your personal goal. Why is the goal important to you? What changes will happen in your life if you reach this goal?

2. **Motivation Behind the Goal:**

   ○ Explain about what made you decide to set this goal. Was it based on a personal wish, a challenge, an experience, or an aim?

3. **Planning and Initial Steps:**

   ○ Show how you planned to reach your goal and what steps you've already taken. How did you start, and what were the first things you did?Show how you planned to reach your goal and what steps you've already taken. How did you start, and what were the first things you did?

4. Strategies and Approaches:

- Briefly explain the plans and strategies you're using to reach your objective. Are you following a certain plan or method? How do you organize your work and decide what to do first?

5. Challenges and Obstacles:

- Carefully consider any problems or challenges you have faced or expect to face. Describe how you plan to get past these problems and what changes you have made to your approach.

6. Progress and Milestones:

- Tell what you've done to reach your goal so far. Have you reached any important points? What are some things you can be proud of?

7. Learning and Adaptation:

- Share about what this process has taught you about yourself. How have you changed the way you do things based on what you've learned?

8. Support and Resources:

- Acknowledge any help or resources that have been very important to you on your journey. This could be people, things, classes, or even habits.

9. Looking Ahead:

- Be mindful about the next steps you want to take and any plans you have for the future. How do you keep yourself going and your mind on your goal?

10. Concluding Thoughts:

- Finally, share your thoughts on how important it is to set and work toward personal goals. What has this trip taught you or changed about you?

CHAPTER 60

CROSSROADS OF CHOICE

Objective:

W RITE A STORY ABOUT A time when you had to make a tough choice. Focus on the things you thought about, the choice you made, and the result of that choice.

Guidelines:

1. **Context of the Decision:**

   ○ Put the hard choice in its proper context to begin with. What was going on, and why was making the choice hard? What did the stakes look like?

2. **Options and Considerations:**

   ○ Describe the choices you had. What did you think about when you were deciding between these options? Were there moral problems, personal beliefs, or real-world effects at play?

3. **Emotional State and Influence:**

   ○ During the decision-making process, think about how you feel. What emotions did you feel that affected how you made your choice? Were you looking for advice or going with your gut?

4. **The Decision:**

   ○ Describe the decision-making moment. What did you decide in the end?

How did you come to this decision? What drove you?

5. Immediate Aftermath:

○ Explain what happened right after you made your choice. How did you feel when you finished? What were the first effects or reactions?

6. Long-Term Outcome:

○ Talk about what the decision will mean in the long run. What changes did it make in your life, relationships, or job? Was the result what you expected, or did it have effects you didn't expect?

7. Lessons Learned:

○ Think about what you learned by making this choice. What changes have you made in the way you make decisions in the future?

8. Personal Growth:

○ Feel free to think about how this experience helped you grow as a person. Do you see or understand yourself and other people differently now?

9. Concluding Thoughts:

○ Finally, describe what you think about the experience as a whole. What new information have you learned, and how do these new ideas affect how you make decisions now?

10. Advice to Others:

○ If you can, give advice to people who might have to make the same choice. Based on what you've seen, what would you suggest?

CHAPTER 61

THE DAY OF TRUE WORDS

Objective:

W RITE A CREATIVE AND fun story about a day when the main character's predictions come true, and look at the funny, strange, and sometimes crazy things that happen.

Guidelines:

1. **Introduction of the Magical Day**:

   ○ Set up the unusual premise first. The main character finds out that their words can become real in what way? Is it a surprise, a wish come true, or a strange event?

2. **Early Discoveries**:

   ○ Describe how the main character first reacts and tries out their newfound power. What are the first things they prove to be true by accident?

3. **Fun and Whimsical Escapades**:

   ○ Come up with a bunch of silly and fun things that happen when the main character's words come true. They can be anything from funny misunderstandings to nice surprises.

4. **Impact on Daily Life**:

○ Find out how this ability changes the main character's daily life. How do people interact with each other at home, school, or work when these strange things happen?

5. Learning to Navigate the Power:

○ Show how the character is learning to handle their power. Do they start to think about what they say more, or do they welcome the chaos?

6. Unexpected Twists:

○ Add challenges or twists that you didn't anticipate. What happens when the main character says something that causes problems they didn't mean to?

7. Interactions with Others:

○ Describe how you interact with friends, family, or strangers who are affected by the strange events. How do these interactions add to the day's chaos or humor?

8. Climactic Event:

○ Build up to a big event that happens because of what the main character says. This could be a big comedy mistake or a moment when you realize how powerful words can be.

9. Resolution:

○ Finish with how the magical day turned out. Does the power wear off, or does the main character figure out a way to undo what it does? What do they learn about how to talk to each other and how powerful words are?

10. Reflective Ending:

○ At the end, have the main character think about their amazing day. How has the event changed the way they think about the words they use?

CHAPTER 62

CHATTER IN THE ANIMAL KINGDOM

Objective:

M AKE UP A HUMOROUS and imaginative story about a world where animals can talk. The story should focus on their conversations, interactions, and the different points of view they offer.

Guidelines:

1. **Introduction of the Talking Animals:**

   ○ Start off by talking about the idea of a world where animals can talk. In what ways do people and animals themselves see this ability? Is it a normal part of the world, or is it something new?

2. **Diverse Animal Characters:**

   ○ Add a variety of different animal characters. Give them unique personalities that are in line with their species. Like a wise old owl, a chatty squirrel, or a lion who stands tall.

3. **Setting the Scene:**

   ○ Set up the scenes in a forest, a farm, a city park, or a household, all of which are places where these conversations happen. What effects do these settings have on the interactions?

4. **Animal Conversations and Topics**:

- Make conversations that show things from the animals' points of view. What do they speak about? This could be about something as simple as food and the weather, or it could be about something more meaningful or funny.

5. **Inter-species Dynamics**:

- Discover more about how different species interact with each other. How do prey and predators talk to each other? Is there confusion or a moment of clarity?

6. **Human and Animal Interactions**:

- How do people interact with or talk to animals when they are around? What special situations come up because of this ability to talk?

7. **Adventures or Misadventures**:

- Add a series of adventures or misadventures that are based on what the animals are saying. This could help people without them knowing it, solve problems, or make things more interestingly chaotic.

8. **Moral or Lesson**:

- Keep the tone light and funny, but sneak in a moral or lesson. What can we learn from the animals about nature, getting along with others, or seeing things from different points of view?

9. **Climactic Event**:

- Bring together different animal characters for a big ending. This could be a party, an urge to work together to solve a problem, or a big misunderstanding.

10. **Concluding Reflections**:

- Finish with the animal characters' thoughts on what they said and how they interacted. What have they found out or learned?

CHAPTER 63

ENCHANTMENT ACADEMY

Objective:

WRITE AN IMAGINATIVE AND funny story about a magical school where students learn fun and unusual things. The story should include the students' magical mishaps, adventures, and the school's unique classes.

Guidelines:

1. **Introduction of the Magical School**:

   ○ Start by telling them about the magical school. Describe how it looks, where it is, and any magical abilities it has that aren't found anywhere else. And how is this school different from other schools?

2. **Diverse Range of Magical Subjects**:

   ○ Identify the different fun and interesting subjects that the school teaches. Some of these are making potions, enchanted art, taking care of mythical creatures, casting spells, and studying magical plants.

3. **Main Characters - Students and Teachers**:

   ○ Address the main characters, who could be students or teachers. Give them unique personalities and magical skills or hobbies.

4. A Typical Day at School:

- What does a typical day look like at this magical school? Describe the classes. What do the students and teachers do together? Add scenes to a number of unusual classes.

5. Unique Challenges and Projects:

- Include challenges or projects that are only done by students in your classes. This could be an odd assignment, a mysterious school-wide project, or a magical tournament.

6. Magical Mishaps and Adventures:

- Add magical mishaps and adventures to the story. What happens when a magic creature gets away or a spell goes wrong?

7. Friendships and Rivalries:

- Find out how the students' friendships and rivalries work. In their studies of magic, how do they work together or against each other?

8. Special Event or Problem:

- Write about an important event or problem that happens at the school. This could be a scary event, a magical festival, or a puzzle that the students need to solve.

9. Climactic Resolution:

- Eventually get the whole school involved. There are many possible outcomes for this: the end of the special event, the solution to the problem, or a grand magical show.

10. Concluding Lessons and Growth:

- At the end, have the characters think about what they've been through. How have they grown as people, friends, and through magic?

CHAPTER 64

SWEET ADVENTURE IN CANDYLAND

Objective:

W RITE A FUN AND creative story about an adventure in a magical land where everything is made of candy. The story should show the world's wonders, challenges, and unique features.

Guidelines:

1. **Introduction to the Candyland**:

    ○ Start by telling about the magical land of candy. How does it look? What kinds of candy are the buildings, plants, and landscape? Is it a rainbow of colors, or is it based on a certain kind of candy?

2. **Main Characters**:

    ○ Show us the characters who are starting the adventure. Living in the candy world, or just finding it by chance? What drives and characterizes them?

3. **The Start of the Adventure**:

    ○ Prepare for the adventure. What duty or goal do the characters have? Are they on the hunt for a legendary candy, trying to save someone, or exploring Candyland's uncharted areas?

4. **Whimsical Obstacles and Challenges**:

   ○ Make up ridiculous problems and challenges for the characters to face. There could be chocolate rivers, marshmallow swamps, or gumdrop mountains on this list.

5. **Interactions with Candyland Residents**:

   ○ Include discussions with the people who live in Candyland. What kind of bugs live in that candy? They help or hurt the characters' journey in what ways?

6. **Discovery of Unique Candy Phenomena**:

   ○ Have the characters find out about strange and magical candy effects. This could be a licorice forest that changes shape, a kingdom of gummy bears, or a strange peppermint wind that changes the world.

7. **Themes of Friendship and Teamwork**:

   ○ Add ideas of sharing, working together, and friendship. By working together, how do the characters get through tough situations? What do they learn about making friends and sharing treats?

8. **Climactic Moment**:

   ○ Build up to a major turning point in the story. This could mean finding the legendary candy, getting past a big problem, or facing off against a sour lemon warlock for the last time.

9. **Resolution and Return**:

   ○ At the end of the adventure, the characters should have either reached their goal or gone home. How does the trip changed them or the way they think about candy?

10. **Reflective Ending**:

   ○ Leave with a thought about the adventure. What memories do the characters hold dear? How are they going to remember or go back to the magical Candyland?

CHAPTER 65

GATEWAY TO ANOTHER WORLD

Objective:

W RITE A STORY IN your thoughts about a person who finds a strange door in their backyard that leads to a different world. Show the adventures and problems they face.

Guidelines:

1. **Discovery of the Door:**

    ○ Create a situation where the character finds the door to begin. How does it get hidden or shown? What does the character think about this strange find at first?

2. **First Passage Through the Door:**

    ○ Describe the character's preference to go through the door and their first experience in the parallel world. What changes do they notice immediately?

3. **Description of the Parallel Universe:**

    ○ Express the parallel universe in vivid detail. How does the world's landscape, people, and natural or physical laws differ from the character's own?

4. **Encounters and Interactions:**

○ Describe the people or creatures that the main character meets in the parallel universe. Are they friendly, mean, or not interested? What does the main character say and do with them?

5. **Exploration and Adventure**:

○ Describe how the main protagonist explores and has adventures in the parallel universe. How do they get around, and where do they go that is different?

6. **Purpose or Quest in the New World**:

○ Make sure the main character in the parallel universe has a goal or quest to complete. Looking for answers, trying to help someone, or trying to get back home are all possible goals.

7. **Overcoming Challenges**:

○ Outline the character's problems or struggles and how they solve them. This could mean figuring out puzzles, staying out of harm's way, or learning about the culture of the new world.

8. **Parallel Universe's Impact on the Character**:

○ Think about how the main character's time in the parallel universe changed them. What do they learn or how do things change for them?

9. **Returning to the Original World**:

○ Choose whether the character goes back to their original world and how they do it. What about them or their surroundings has changed because of their journey?

10. **Concluding Reflections**:

○ At the end, have the character think about what a wonderful time was like. How has finding the parallel universe changed the way they think about life?

CHAPTER 66

THE ADVENTURES OF TROUBLESOME WHISKERS

Objective:

W RITE AN ENTERTAINING AND light-hearted story about a cat named Whiskers who gets into all sorts of trouble and makes people laugh.

Guidelines:

1. **Introduction of the Mischievous Cat:**

   ○ Start by introducing Whiskers, the cat. Its personality traits, appearance, and mischievous nature should all be described. How is Whiskers a troublemaker?

2. **Setting the Scene:**

   ○ Imagine that Whiskers lives there. Is it a farm, a cozy house, or a row of busy houses? How does this scenario make it possible to get into trouble?

3. **First Escapade:**

   ○ Introduce with Whiskers's first adventure. This could be something funny, like stealing food, pulling pranks on the family dog, or making a mess in the house.

4. **Reaction of Family or Neighbors:**

○ Show how people around Whiskers are reacting. Are they annoyed, amused, or simply unaware of its antics? When the cat gets into trouble, how do they handle it?

5. **Escalating Adventures**:

○ Come up with a series of problems or adventures that Whiskers gets into. These could include exploring the neighborhood, meeting other animals, or getting involved in human activities by accident.

6. **Whiskers's Unique Tactics**:

○ To get into trouble, talk about Whiskers's clever or unique behaviors. What moves or strategies does it use that make it stand out?

7. **Comical Consequences**:

○ Make sure that the outcome of every adventure are funny and lighthearted. How do these things end up making people laugh or bringing them together?

8. **A Moment of Heroism**:

○ Add a twist where Whiskers's mischievous behavior makes him a hero by accident, like when he stops a burglary or rescues another animal.

9. **Resolution and Acceptance**:

○ The family or neighbors should accept Whiskers's mischievousness as a fun part of their life by the end. What last behavior solidifies its place in the people?

10. **Reflective Ending**:

○ Lastly, think about how Whiskers makes people happy and makes them laugh, even though it can be a pain.

CHAPTER 67

A DAY OF POWER

Objective:

I MAGINE WAKING UP WITH a superpower that lasts only one day. Write a story about the fun, the problems, and the decisions that can be made with this temporary power.

Guidelines:

1. **Discovery of the Superpower**:

   ○ Start with the primary character (you) waking up and finding out they have superpowers. How do you know you have it? Is it a power you've always wanted, or is it something you didn't expect?

2. **Understanding the Power**:

   ○ Describe the first things you did in order to understand and manage the power. What can it do and what are its limits? Feeling good or bad about having this power?

3. **First Use of the Power**:

   ○ Describe the first time you used your superpower. Is it used to get something for yourself, to help someone, or just for fun? What do the people around respond immediately?

4. **Moral Dilemma**:

○ Create a moral problem or choice about how to utilize the power. Do you keep it a secret, mention it to everyone, or use it to deal with a problem or challenge?

5. **Adventures and Encounters**:

○ Arrange a day's worth of encounters or events that all have something to do with using the superpower. This can be anything from fun and amusing to serious and challenging.

6. **Impact on Others**:

○ Find how the things you can do with your superpower change the people around you. Does it change relationships, lead to misunderstandings, or have effects that were not expected?

7. **Personal Reflection and Growth**:

○ Think about how you're feeling and what you're thinking throughout the day. What would you think about everyday life, responsibility, and power if you had superpowers for a day?

8. **Climactic Use of the Power**:

○ Build up to a massive moment where the superpower is used in a big way. This could be a brave thing to do, a tough choice, or a sacrifice.

9. **Losing the Power**:

○ Describe the moment when the superpower goes away. How do you feel about things getting back to normal? What's different about you now?

10. **Concluding Reflections**:

○ Finalize with your thoughts on the experience. What did the day you had superpowers teach you? What changes have you seen in yourself and your abilities regarding it?

CHAPTER 68

A VISITOR FROM THE STARS

Objective:

W RITE A FASCINATING AND amusing story about meeting a friendly alien visitor to Earth and the adventures that happen because of their interest in the planet.

Guidelines:

1. **First Encounter**:

   ○ Start with the protagonist character's first meeting with the alien. Give details about where and how they meet. Do they meet by chance in a remote area, or does the alien go out of their way to find the main character?

2. **Alien's Appearance and Personality**:

   ○ Show how the alien looks like, how it acts, and how it talks. What around them makes them clearly not human? Show that they are interested and friendly.

3. **Alien's Fascination with Earth**:

   ○ Show the alien's interest in Earth. In what ways do they find the planet and human society the most interesting or confusing?

4. **Exchange of Knowledge**:

   ○ Come up with a conversation or interaction where the main character and the alien share information about their worlds. How does the protagonist learn about the aliens' culture and where they come from?

5. Adventure on Earth:

○ While the main character states the alien around, make up a series of adventures or explorations. This could include things that aliens have never done before, natural wonders, or cultural experiences.

6. Bonding and Friendship:

○ Demonstrate how the main character and the alien are becoming closer and friends. How do they connect even though they are different? What do they learn about each other or what attracts them both?

7. Teaching and Learning Moments:

○ Tell the alien about Earth and its traditions while the main character talks about their own experiences in space.

8. Help from the Alien:

○ Think about how the alien could help the main character or the community by using their advanced technology or knowledge.

9. Farewell and Impact:

○ Prepare for the alien departure. What is their way of saying goodbye? What changes the main character and how they see the world after the encounter?

10. Reflective Conclusion:

○ At the end, have the main character think about what happened. What has meeting the alien taught them about life, people, and the endlessness of the universe?

ADVENTURES IN THE PAGES

Objective:

WRITE A FASCINATING THRILLER about a character who can magically jump into books and live out the stories inside them. Explore different literary worlds and how these adventures impact the character.

Guidelines:

1. **Discovery of the Power**:

   ○ Start with the character finding that they can jump into books. How does this take place? Is it a magical gift, a mysterious inheritance, or something that was found by accident?

2. **First Book Adventure**:

   ○ Give the first book that the character picks up. What do they do when they realize they are part of the story? What kind of book is it, and what part do they play in the story?

3. **Exploring Different Genres**:

   ○ Give the character to read a variety of different types of books. They could pick up a classic adventure, a romance, a mystery, or a huge fantasy story. How do these various types of music affect them?

4. Interaction with Book Characters:

- Describe how you interact with popular characters from the books. What do these characters do when they see the main character? Does the main character change how the story goes?

5. Challenges and Conflicts:

- Bring up challenges or troubles that the character faces in the book worlds. Do they find it hard to fit in, are they in danger in the stories, or do they have to deal with the moral issues that come up when stories are changed?

6. Learning and Growth:

- Explain how the events in the books help the character grow as a person. What do they learn from having a variety of experiences?

7. Impact on Real Life:

- Find out what happens in the characters' real life after the adventures in the books. Do they realize their world better, learn new skills, or get a new perspective on it?

8. Climactic Adventure:

- Prepare the character for a big adventure that will test them in ways they didn't expect. In this case, the book world might be extremely challenging or dangerous.

9. Decision to Continue or Stop:

- Your character should have to make a choice about their power. Does this happen again and again, or do they decide to stop?

10. Concluding Reflections:

- Wrap up with the character thinking about their amazing experiences. What new ways do their stories, imaginations, and experiences in the pages make them feel?

CHAPTER 70

THE WHIMSICAL CALENDAR

Objective:

WRITE AN ENJOYABLE AND imaginative story about a world where every day has a different, fantastical theme. Show how the people who live there deal with and enjoy these themes that change all the time.

Guidelines:

1. **Introduction to the World**:

   ○ Start off by telling them about this unique world. Explain the basic rules and how the daily themes are chosen. Is it a magical event, a long-standing tradition, or something that happens naturally in the world?

2. **Examples of Daily Themes**:

   ○ Provide scenarios of the different themes that happen every day. Several concepts are Backwards Day, Upside-Down Day, Colorful Day, and more creative ones are Miniature Day and Flying Day.

3. **Main Character's Experience**:

   ○ Describe your main character and how they get through these themed days. Are they excited, stressed out, or good at adjusting? How do they get ready for each day?

4. **Daily Life and Activities**:

   ○ Describe the things you do and how you live your daily life that are related
     to the themes. Show how the theme of the day affects your work, school,
     and free time.

5. **Challenges and Fun Moments**:

   ○ Make use of challenges and fun things that go with the themes. How do
     the characters deal with problems or take advantage of the new chances that
     come up every day?

6. **Interaction Among Characters**:

   ○ Include how the characters talk to each other as they go through the themed
     days together. How do these themes change how people talk to each other,
     interact, and do social things?

7. **A Special or Unexpected Day**:

   ○ Add a unique or unexpected theme day that changes the plot. In what ways
     do the characters respond to a theme they haven't seen or heard before?

8. **Learning and Adaptation**:

   ○ Show how the main character grows and changes every day. How do they
     come up with creative plans or solutions?

9. **Impact on the Community**:

   ○ Find out what impact these themed days have on the neighborhood or on
     society as entirety. Do they bring people together, make them think of new
     ideas, or make things funny?

10. **Concluding Reflection**:

   ○ At the end, leave the main character think about what it means to live in
     a world where themes are always changing. How do they feel about this
     fast-paced way of life? What have they learned?

CHAPTER 71

A JOURNEY OF CULTURAL DISCOVERY

Objective:

W RITE A STORY WHERE the main character learns about and gains knowledge of a culture that is different from their own. The story must discover themes of acceptance, empathy, and the richness of cultural diversity.

Guidelines:

1. **Introduction of the Main Character**:

   ○ Start by describing us about the primary character and where they come from. What culture do they come from, and how have they been exposed to other cultures so far?

2. **Catalyst for Cultural Discovery**:

   ○ Give the character a reason or event that makes them want to learn about another culture. It could be a new friend, a school project, a trip, or an event in the community.

3. **First Impressions and Misunderstandings**:

   ○ Write about how the character felt about the new culture at first. Write down any misunderstandings, biases, or ideas they already have.

4. Learning Process:

○ Show the character is learning about the culture by doing activities. This involves going to cultural events, trying new foods, learning a language, or reading about the history and traditions of the culture.

5. Building Relationships:

○ Include building relationships with people from the other culture. The character understands and appreciates things more after these interactions.

6. Challenges and Realizations:

○ Reveal the problems that the character has to deal with on their journey. There could be problems with communication, misunderstandings of other cultures, or having to face their own presumptions.

7. Moments of Empathy and Inclusion:

○ Point out times when the character understands and sympathizes with others. How can they learn to value and respect differences between cultures?

8. Impact of the Cultural Experience:

○ Think about how the character's cultural experience has changed them. How does it change the way they think about differences, community, and what they are?

9. Sharing the Experience:

○ Think about how the character communicates other people about what they've learned. Do they start to speak out for cultural understanding and acceptance in their own community?

10. Concluding Reflection:

○ End with the character thinking about their journey of learning about other cultures. What lessons have they learned about diversity, empathy, and how important it is to accept other cultures?

CHAPTER 72

NEW HORIZONS

Objective:

Write a story about someone who moves to a new country and the problems they face, the changes they have to make to fit in with the new culture, and their journey of adapting and discovering new things.

Guidelines:

1. **Character Introduction and Background**:

    ○ Start by introducing the character and telling us why they are moving to a new country. Where did they come from, and why are they moving? Is it for work, school, fun, getting away, or family?

2. **Initial Impressions and Challenges**:

    ○ Describe the character's initial perceptions when they get to the new country. What problems do they have to deal with at first? Think about problems like language barriers, cultural differences, homesickness, or getting around.

3. **Cultural Learning and Adaptation**:

    ○ Show how the character learns about and adjusts to the new culture. How do they deal with daily tasks, traditions, and societal standards?

4. **Building Relationships**:

○ Include details about how the character attempt to meet people in the new country. Finding a community, making friends, or connecting with coworkers are all examples of this.

5. Overcoming Setbacks:

○ Add issues or challenges that the character faces and how they deal with them. These problems could be misunderstandings caused by cultural differences, loneliness, or getting used to new social roles.

6. Moments of Joy and Discovery:

○ Highlight times of happiness, discovery, and success. Display instances in which the character learns to value the new culture, enjoys distinctive features of the country, or completes a personal objective.

7. Cultural Exchange and Contribution:

○ Find out what the character brings to the cultural exchange and what they learn from it. In what ways do they share their culture and accept the new one?

8. Personal Growth and Reflection:

○ Think about how the character grows as a person. What changes about their view of life, themselves, and the world when they move to a new country?

9. Integration and Acceptance:

○ Visualize how the character fits in with their new surroundings. Having a place to belong or making a new home for themselves is important.

10. Concluding Thoughts:

○ At the end, have the character think about their journey. What did they learn, and how do they feel about their new life in the country?

Chapter 73

PATHWAY TO EMPATHY

Objective:

W RITE A STORY ABOUT a character who is trying to understand and practice empathy. Show their experiences, problems, and how empathy has changed their life and relationships.

Guidelines:

1. **Character Introduction**:

   ○ Start by introducing the main character. At first, they might not care about others, be self-centered, or not be able to see things from other people's points of view. How do they feel about other people's thoughts and feelings?

2. **Inciting Incident**:

   ○ Add something that makes the main character think differently than they usually do. It could be a loss of a loved one, a major setback, or meeting someone from a very different background.

3. **Gradual Understanding**:

   ○ Show how the character learns to care about others over time. How can they start to see things from other people's points of view? Include situations when you think about yourself and realize things.

4. **Experiences that Foster Empathy**:

○ Describe events that help the protagonist feel empathy. This might mean doing things like volunteering, making new friends, or being in situations where they need help and understanding from other people.

5. **Challenges and Resistance:**

○ Bring in problems or opposition that the character has to deal with in order to develop empathy. This could include problems inside the person, misunderstandings, or disagreements with other people.

6. **Moment of Deep Empathy:**

○ Make a turning point where the character really feels empathy. That person might really connect with someone else's feelings in this situation.

7. **Impact on Relationships:**

○ See how the character's newly acquired ability to understand how others feel affects their relationships. What changes in the way they talk to their family, friends, and coworkers?

8. **Empathy Leading to Action:**

○ Show that the character did something because they cared. This could mean standing up for someone, helping someone in need, or changing a behavior that hurts other people.

9. **Personal Growth:**

○ Think about how the character has changed as they've learned to understand others. What's different? What do they know about other people and themselves?

10. **Concluding Reflections:**

○ In the end, have the main character think about how important and powerful empathy is. How will they keep showing empathy and how will they spread it?

CHAPTER 74

THE INCLUSIVITY CLUB

Objective:

W RITE A STORY ABOUT someone who starts an inclusive club at school. The story should focus on what drives them, the problems they face, and how the club affects the rest of the school.

Guidelines:

1. **Character Introduction**:

   ○ Start by introducing the main character. Why do they want to start a club for acceptance? This could be because of their own experiences, seeing unfair things happen, or wanting to make the world a better place.

2. **Initial Planning and Goals**:

   ○ Describe how the club initially developed. What do the club's goals and plans look like? How does the main character set it up?

3. **Gathering Members**:

   ○ Show how to get people to join. What does the main character do to get other people to join? Bring interest to how different the members are and why they joined.

4. **First Club Meeting**:

- Describe the first meeting of the club. What kinds of talks happen? What does the main character do to lead and run the meeting?

5. **Challenges and Obstacles**:

- List the problems the club has to deal with. There may be doubts from other students, problems with logistics, or disagreements within the club.

6. **Club Activities and Initiatives**:

- List the things that the club does and the projects that it works on. These could be workshops, worthwhile events, campaigns to raise awareness, or projects that help people in the community.

7. **Impact on the School Community**:

- Show how the club has changed the school community. How does it change people's minds, help them understand, or make real changes?

8. **Personal Growth of the Protagonist**:

- Think about the main character's growth as a person. What do they learn about being a leader, speaking out, and including everyone?

9. **Response from Peers and Faculty**:

- What did your peers and teachers think? What do other people at school think about the club's work?

10. **Concluding Reflections**:

- Finish with the main character's thought about the club's journey and what they've accomplished. Are they optimistic about the club's and school's culture's future?

This guide will help you write a story about the ups and downs of starting an inclusivity club. It will stress how important it is to have empathy, understand, and take action to make the world a better place for everyone.

CHAPTER 75

UNITED FOR A CAUSE

Objective:

W RITE A STORY ABOUT characters from different backgrounds working together to reach a common goal. The story should explore themes of unity, diversity, cooperation, and the value of different points of view.

Guidelines:

1. **Introduction of Diverse Characters**:

   ○ Start by describing about the characters. They all come from different places. This diversity can include differences in race, culture, socioeconomic status, and location, as well as differences in personality and skills.

2. **Setting the Common Goal**:

   ○ Figure out what these characters have in common that brings them together. This could be a cause they all care about, a team competition, a community project, or a mission they all work jointly on.

3. **Initial Challenges and Differences**:

   ○ Highlight the problems they face at first because they are different. There may be misunderstandings, different ideas, or problems communicating.

4. **Learning and Understanding**:

- Let the characters learn about each other's pasts and points of view. How do they start to see how different they are and value those differences?

5. **Building Trust and Cooperation**:

- Describe how the characters learn to trust each other and work together. Include times when people work together, compromise, and help each other.

6. **Combining Skills and Knowledge**:

- Show how their different knowledge and skills help them reach their goal. How do their different skills work together to make them better?

7. **Overcoming a Major Obstacle**:

- Add a major challenge or setback that tests their ability to work together and stay determined. How can they work together to get through it?

8. **Deepening Relationships**:

- Look into how the characters' relationships are getting stronger. How do they go from being friends with a common goal to becoming a group that works together?

9. **Achieving the Goal**:

- Build up to the stage where they reach their goal. How does their success come from being united and different as well?

10. **Reflecting on the Journey**:

- Close with the characters thinking about their journey. What did they learn about working with oddballs? What modifications did the experience make?

CHAPTER 76

TURNING THE TIDE ON BULLYING

Objective:

W RITE A NARRATIVE THAT looks into the problem of bullying by focusing on the experiences of those who are bullied and ending on a positive note that encourages understanding, growth, and transformation.

Guidelines:

1. **Introduction of Characters and Setting**:

   - Start by introducing the main characters, such as the bully, the victim, and any friends or bystanders. Place the scene somewhere you know well, like a school, neighborhood, or online platform.

2. **Incidents of Bullying**:

   - Describe instances where bullying occurs. These should be based on real events and show how the victim felt without being too graphic.

3. **The Victim's Perspective**:

   - Find out how the victim feels and what they did. How does the bullying change their life, relationships, and sense of self-worth?

4. **Bystanders' Reactions**:

○ Include spectators' viewpoints. Are they doing nothing, getting involved, or not sure what to do? How does their response make things worse or better?

5. Insight into the Bully's Motivations:

○ Provide information about the bully's background and what drives them. What makes them act the way they do? This knowledge shouldn't make the behavior okay, but it should give you more information.

6. Intervention and Support:

○ Add some kind of help or assistance. Someone like a teacher, counselor, friend, or family member could step in and support.

7. Path to Resolution:

○ Create an approach to reach an outcome. This could mean having an open conversation, using restorative justice, counseling, or for the bully to realize what they're doing and change their mind.

8. Positive Change and Growth:

○ Show how the characters have grown and changed for the better. In what ways do they learn from it? Some examples of this are the bully realizing the effects of their actions and changing how they act, and the victim getting stronger or more support.

9. Rebuilding Relationships:

○ If it makes sense, include establishing or fixing relationships. In what way do the characters move on from the bullying?

10. Concluding Reflection:

○ Finish up by showing How do the characters move on after being bullied?

CHAPTER 77

THE CHAMPION OF FAIRNESS

Objective:

WRITE A TALE ABOUT a character who stands up for someone who is being treated unfairly. Show how brave they are, what problems they face, and how their actions influence others.

Guidelines:

1. Introduction of Characters and Setting:

- Start by introducing the main character and the person who is being harmed. Set the scene to show where and how this unfair treatment takes place.

2. Incident of Unfair Treatment:

- Describe the event where the unfair treatment takes place. What is going on and why is it not fair? Make sure that this portrayal strikes the reader as unfair.

3. Protagonist's Initial Reaction:

- Describe how the main individual initially reacted when they saw how unfair things were. In what ways does it make them feel? Surprise, anger, or sympathy?

4. Decision to Take a Stand:

- Guide the main character to decide what to do. Why do they do what they do? Do they have a personal belief, a sense of what's right, or a connection to the person who is being mistreated?

5. Action to Address the Unfairness:

- Show what the main lead does to deal with the problem. Do they talk to the person who hurt them, ask for help, or help the victim?

6. Challenges and Consequences:

- Face challenges or consequences with your primary protagonist for standing up. This could be internal doubts, pushback from peers, or misunderstandings from people in power.

7. Support from Others:

- Include help from other characters. Who looks out for the primary character? How do they help or support them?

8. Impact of Standing Up:

- Summarize how the main character's actions affected things. What effects does it have on the person being mistreated, the community as a whole, and the main character?

9. Character Growth and Reflection:

- Think about how the centerpiece of the story has changed because of this event. What do they learn about themselves, about justice, and about how powerful it is to stand up for other people?

10. Concluding Resolution:

- End the story with a resolution that reinforces the message. What has changed because of what the main character did? How do they feel about what they did?

CHAPTER 78

THE MOSAIC OF DIFFERENCES

Objective:

C REATE A STORY ABOUT diversity, empathy, and the beauty of a diverse community that shows how important it is to understand and accept the differences between people.

Guidelines:

1. **Diverse Group of Characters**:

   ○ Add characters to the story who are different from each other in terms of culture, background, personality, or skills. These differences should be at the heart of how the story develops.

2. **Setting that Brings Characters Together**:

   ○ Set up a place where these different characters can meet. It could be a school project, a neighborhood event, or the place where you work.

3. **Initial Misunderstandings or Conflicts**:

   ○ Start by showing how the characters' differences cause problems, misunderstandings, or challenges. Which of these first interactions shows a lack of acceptance or understanding?

4. Journey to Understanding:

○ Make the story more interesting by showing how the characters learn to understand each other. This could include having the same experiences, having open conversations, or being in situations where you need to work together.

5. Challenges Along the Way:

○ Include challenges and setbacks that are true to life in the characters' journey. What do they do to get around these problems? The process teaches what lessons!

6. Moments of Empathy and Connection:

○ During these times, you should emphasize when the characters show empathy and actual connections. How do these events reduce barriers and alter how people see things?

7. Celebration of Differences:

○ Show how the characters learn to enjoy what makes them unique. Show what's good about having different people in the group.

8. Resolution of Conflicts:

○ Solve initial problems in a way that shows how the characters have changed and grown. In what ways have their relationships and attitudes changed?

9. Impact on the Wider Community:

○ Increase the length of the story to demonstrate how this acceptance has affected the larger community. How does the group's change affect the people around them?

10. Concluding Reflection:

○ Finally, think about how important it is to understand and accept differences. In what way does the story teach us about diversity and understanding?

CHAPTER 79

EMBRACING UNIQUENESS

Objective:

C REATE A STORY ABOUT a character who learns to appreciate and embrace their unique qualities, quirks, and personal background as they go on a journey of self-discovery.

Guidelines:

1. **Character Introduction and Initial Struggle:**

   ○ Start by introducing the main character and focusing on how they are struggling with who they are at the beginning. Insecure or uncomfortable about what parts of themselves do they feel this way? Is it the way they look, the things they like, their culture, or their personality?

2. **Inciting Incident:**

   ○ Describe an event or situation that starts the main character's path to accepting themselves. It could be a challenge, a new place, or meeting someone who makes them think about things in a new way.

3. **Encounters and Experiences:**

   ○ Summarize the events and interactions that make the character think about who they are. You should include both good and bad experiences that help them understand.

4. Role Models or Mentors:

- ○ Find friends, mentors, or role models who like the main individual just the way they are. How do these people affect how the main character sees themselves?

5. Overcoming Challenges:

- ○ Demonstrate how the character deals with and gets through problems that are connected to who they are. How do these problems help them feel better about who they are?

6. Moments of Doubt and Reflection:

- ○ Include moments of doubt and ideology. How does the main character struggle with how they feel about who they are?

7. Realization and Acceptance:

- ○ Bring the character to a point where they realize and accept what's going on. What event or realization helps them fully accept what makes them special?

8. Positive Changes:

- ○ Present how the character's life has changed for the better since they were accepted. What changes in their relationships, confidence, and choices when they accept who they are?

9. Impact on Others:

- ○ Investigate how the main character's journey affects the people around them. Do they make other people want to accept themselves?

10. Concluding Reflection:

- ○ At the end, have the main character think about their journey. What have they learned about themselves and how important it is to be proud of who you are?

CHAPTER 80

BRIDGES OF FRIENDSHIP

Objective:

WRITE THE STORY ABOUT how characters from different cultures become close friends and how they get past prejudices and misunderstandings.

Guidelines:

1. **Introduction of Characters from Different Cultures**:

   ○ Start off by introducing the main characters, who all come from different cultures. Describe their first thoughts and the cultural setting in which they lived.

2. **First Encounter and Challenges**:

   ○ Define their first meeting and the problems they have trying to understand each other. Some examples of this are language barriers, misunderstandings about culture, or biases that people already have.

3. **Shared Experiences**:

   ○ Create a story where the characters share events that bring them closer together. They may need to work together on a project, because they share an interest, or because they need to.

4. **Learning About Each Other's Cultures**:

○ Show how the characters are interested in getting to know each other's cultures. This could mean sharing their cultures, taking part in each other's traditions, or having open conversations about their pasts.

5. Overcoming Misconceptions:

○ Show how the characters get over their biases and misconceptions about each other's cultures. How do these new facts make their friendship stronger?

6. Mutual Support and Understanding:

○ Highlight situations when people helped each other and understood each other. Some problems they face are personal and cultural. How do they help each other?

7. Celebrating Diversity:

○ Express how the characters value and enjoy their differences in culture, and how this makes their friendship stronger. This could be a cultural fusion event, a joint venture that brings together people from different backgrounds, or just enjoying the different kinds of people they are friends with.

8. Facing and Overcoming a Conflict Together:

○ Bring up a problem or conflict that puts their friendship to the test. How do they deal with this together, and what part does their knowledge of each other's cultures play?

9. Impact on Their Communities:

○ Find out how their friendship impacts their own social groups or communities. Do they get rid of barriers or change how people think?

10. Concluding Reflections on Friendship:

○ At the conclusion of the story, have the characters think about how important and powerful their friendship is. What have they learned about getting along, friendship, and other cultures?

CHAPTER 81

THE COLLABORATIVE TALE

Objective:

H AVE A CREATIVE STORYTELLING activity where friends write paragraphs of a story together, building on each other's ideas to make a fun and believable story.

Guidelines:

1. **Choose a Starting Point**:

   ○ Get started by giving the story a basic idea or scene. Pick a theme or genre, such as comedy, adventure, mystery, or other. The first author begins with a paragraph that sets the scene.

2. **Building the Story**:

   ○ The next person in the round-robin adds a paragraph that builds on the one that came before it. They should try to keep the story going, make the characters better, or add new things that fit with the story's direction.

3. **Character Development**:

   ○ Each person who writes the story should help to make the characters more real as it goes on. Describe their goals, the problems they face, and how they interact with the setting or other characters.

4. **Plot Advancements**:

- Every paragraph should try to move the story along. Include problems, surprises, or events that move the story along and keep it interesting.

5. **Maintaining Continuity**:

- Each writer should keep the flow of previous paragraphs in mind while adding their own creative ideas. It is important to keep up with how the story is going and who the characters are.

6. **Embracing Creativity**:

- Encourage every individual to share their own unique thoughts and ideas. The fun of a round-robin story is that you can't be sure what will happen next and everyone can be creative.

7. **Flexible Story Direction**:

- Be ready for the story to go in ways you didn't expect. The fun of reading is discovering where the story goes, and each author may have their own ideas.

8. **Concluding the Story**:

- Pick a point where the story is going to conclude. The last person to work on it should try to wrap up the story, settle any disagreements, and give it a satisfying ending.

9. **Reflecting on the Experience**:

- When you're done with the story, talk about what was observed. Talk about the best parts, the hardest parts, and what each person liked most about working together.

10. **Sharing or Publishing**:

- You might want to share the finished story with other people or post it in a school magazine, blog, or social media. Celebrate what everyone has done!

CHAPTER 82

THE TWIST AND TURN TALE

Objective:

D O A STORYTELLING ACTIVITY with a group where everyone adds a new twist or character, making the story more interesting and unpredictable.

Guidelines:

1. **Establishing the Basic Storyline**:

   ○ Start with a simple plot or scene to give your story a base. This could be something as simple as a trip, a mystery to solve, or a character's day in the life.

2. **First Contributor's Role**:

   ○ The first contributor sets the scene and provides an introduction to the main characters. The tone and direction of the story should be set by them.

3. **Adding Twists or Characters**:

   ○ Each person who joins adds a new character or a twist to the story. A twist could be a new part of the story, a shocking discovery, or a change in the situation. The story should have new characters that stand out and bring something new to it.

4. **Building on Previous Contributions**:

- Every addition should build on what has already been set up. The participants should keep the story going in the same direction while also adding new parts to it.

5. **Diverse Character Contributions**:

- Encourage people to be creative when they make characters. Characters can have different hobbies, come from different places, and see things from different points of view.

6. **Managing the Plot**:

- As the story goes on, monitor to ensure the plot doesn't get too complicated. People who are taking part should try to add their twists or characters in a way that fits with the rest of the story.

7. **Balancing Narrative Elements**:

- Check the balance of action, dialogue, and description. Each participant should add something to the story to make it more interesting and vibrant.

8. **Concluding the Story**:

- Choose a satisfying ending for the story so that it doesn't go on too long. The last person to contribute should try to bring all the different parts together and come up with a good ending.

9. **Reflecting on the Collaborative Process**:

- Once you're done with the story, think about how you worked together to write it. Talk about the difficulties, your favorite additions, and how each character or plot twist changed the course of the story.

10. **Sharing and Celebrating the Story**:

- You could share the finished story with other people or come up with a creative way to publish it, like in a blog, a school magazine, or a social media post.

CHAPTER 83

CHOOSE YOUR OWN ADVENTURE

Objective:

W RITE AN INTERACTIVE STORY where readers can make decisions at important points that change the character's path and the outcome of the story.

Guidelines:

1. **Story Framework and Setting**:

   o Start by giving your story a compelling structure and setting. This could be a fantasy adventure, a mystery, a sci-fi journey, or any other type of story that can be told in more than one way.

2. **Main Character Introduction**:

   o Describe the main character in a way that makes the reader want to know more. You should give enough background to the character so that they are interesting and believable.

3. **Decision Points**:

   o Figure out where the story's important decisions will be made. The reader gets to decide what the character does next. After making a choice, there should be a clear path with distinct challenges and outcomes.

4. Branching Narratives:

- For each choice, make a story with multiple paths. Make sure that each path has its own interesting characters and events that make it complete on its own.

5. Balancing the Paths:

- Try to find a good balance between the length and difficulty of each path. Although each path may be slightly different, none of them should feel significantly shorter or less developed than the others.

6. Consequences of Choices:

- Make sure that the choices you make have genuine impacts on how the story goes. This makes the reader's choices more important and keeps them interested.

7. Multiple Endings:

- Based on the paths taken, make more than one ending. The choices that are made can lead to very good or extremely undesirable endings.

8. Clues and Foreshadowing:

- Early on in the story, leave hints and foreshadowing that could affect what the reader does later on.

9. Encouraging Replayability:

- Write in a way that makes people want to go in different directions. Each storyline should have enough variety and mystery to make playing it again and again fun.

10. Concluding Each Path:

- Finish each path in a way that makes you pleased. Make sure the reader feels like the story has a happy ending, a lesson learned, or an unexpected twist.

11. Reader Reflection:

○ Give the reader a short time to think about each ending. Find out why they made the decisions they did and how they feel about the outcome.

CHAPTER 84

INSPIRED BEGINNINGS

Objective:

O PEN YOUR STORY WITH a sentence from your favorite book and use it as a starting point for your own story that goes in its own direction.

Guidelines:

1. **Select a Starting Sentence:**

   ○ Pick a strong first sentence from your favorite book. This sentence should be able to lead to a number of different storylines.

2. **Setting and Tone:**

   ○ Set the scene and ambiance of your story. Choose whether to stick with the tone that the first sentence set or go in a different direction.

3. **Develop Original Characters:**

   ○ Give your story its own characters that aren't from the book you're drawing from. Make sure they have unique personalities, histories, and goals.

4. **Crafting the Plot:**

   ○ Make up a story that is different from the source material. Let your story go in its own direction, but use the first sentence as a guide.

5. **Building the World:**

- Figure out how much of the world from the book where the sentence comes from you want to keep. This could be a fantasy or sci-fi book. You can put your story in a totally different world if that works better for your plot.

6. Incorporating Themes:

- Consider the connections between the ideas in the sentence and the ones in the book you like. You can go deeper into similar themes or add new ones that fit with your story.

7. Expanding the Narrative:

- As the story goes on, make sure it becomes its own thing, separate from the book from which the first sentence came.

8. Conflict and Resolution:

- Give your characters an immediate issue or conflict, and build the story towards a solution that fits with the new direction your story is going.

9. Paying Tribute:

- Your story should be unique, but you can honor the book that inspired it in a small way by using tone, theme, or references.

10. Concluding Your Story:

- Finish your story in a way that feels satisfying and fits the story you've created. Make sure it feels complete and separate from the source material.

CHAPTER 85

ALPHABETICAL CHAIN STORY

OBJECTIVE:

Write a cohesive and engaging story where each sentence begins with the successive letter of the alphabet, starting from 'A' and ending with 'Z'.

Guidelines:

1. **A - Starting Point:**

   - Begin your story with a sentence that starts with the letter 'A'. This sentence should set the scene or introduce the main character.

2. **B - Build the Narrative:**

   - The second sentence, starting with 'B', should build upon the first, adding detail to the setting, character, or initiating the plot.

3. **C to M - Developing Plot and Characters:**

   - Continue with sentences for each letter, progressively developing the plot and characters. Ensure each sentence naturally follows from the previous, maintaining the story's flow.

4. **N to T - Climax and Conflict:**

   - Use these letters to build towards the climax of your story. Introduce conflicts, challenges, or key events that drive the plot.

5. **U to Z - Resolution and Conclusion**:

- The final letters should lead to the resolution of the story. Wrap up the narrative, resolve conflicts, and conclude with 'Z' in a satisfying way.

6. **Maintain Cohesiveness**:

- Despite the alphabetical constraint, ensure each sentence contributes to a cohesive and engaging narrative. Avoid forcing the story to fit the letter if it doesn't naturally align.

7. **Creativity with Difficult Letters**:

- Get creative with challenging letters like 'Q', 'X', and 'Z'. Use them as opportunities to introduce unique elements or turns in the story.

8. **Varied Sentence Lengths**:

- Mix up the length and structure of your sentences to keep the story dynamic and interesting.

9. **Review and Refine**:

- After completing the story, review it to ensure it flows logically and smoothly. Refine any parts where the alphabetical constraint may have caused awkward transitions.

10. **Share and Collaborate**:

- Consider making this a collaborative activity with friends or family, where each person contributes a sentence or two. It can be a fun group exercise in creative storytelling.

GUIDED BY OTHERS

Objective:

WRITE A STORY ABOUT a protagonist whose friends or family either directly or indirectly affect the big decisions they have to make in their life. Explore the effects of this kind of influence and the path to becoming independent.

Guidelines:

1. **Character Introduction**:

   ○ Introduce the protagonist and talk about their personality and how much they depend on other people to make decisions. Are they passive, unable to make up their minds, or just used to being told what to do?

2. **Friends and Family Dynamics**:

   ○ Describe how the main character interacts with their family or friends. Who are the important people in their life, and why do they make the choices they do for the main character?

3. **Initial Decisions Made by Others**:

   ○ Start with some important choices that family or friends have already made. These could be about work, relationships, or making choices for yourself. What does the main character do when these choices are made?

4. **Consequences of Decisions**:

○ What will happen as a result of these choices? Are they what make the main character happy, sad, angry, or do something unexpected happen?

5. **Growing Awareness**:

○ Help the main character become more aware of what happens when they don't make their own decisions. What events or realizations bring this to your attention?

6. **Struggle for Autonomy**:

○ Show how hard it is for the main character to become independent. How do they start to stand up for themselves, and what problems do they run into?

7. **Conflict and Resolution**:

○ Make a conflict that comes up considering they want to be independent. This could be a fight with a family member or friend or a time when they have to stick to their own choice.

8. **Character Development**:

○ Use these events to show how the character changes over time. What do they learn and how do they grow, like becoming more confident, assertive, or self-aware?

9. **Turning Point**:

○ Bring the main character to a turning point where they have to make a big choice on their own. What changes about their journey does this choice make?

10. **Concluding Reflections**:

○ At the end, have the main character think about their path to making their own decisions. How have their relationships with family and friends changed over time? What have they learned about making their own decisions and about themselves?

CHAPTER 87

THE FRIENDSHIP CHRONICLES

Objective:

D EVELOP A STORY WITH characters based on your real-life friends. Have each friend give you feedback on the character's traits, actions, and part in the story.

Guidelines:

1. **Gathering Input:**

   ○ First, ask each friend how they'd like to be portrayed. What interests, traits, or habits do they want their character to have? Do they have a certain role or plot they'd like to see?

2. **Character Development:**

   ○ Develop each character based on their words. Make sure that each character fits into the story and shows what their friend is like and what they want.

3. **Setting and Plot:**

   ○ Choose an environment and plot that work for all of your characters. This could be a mystery, an adventure, a fantasy world, or a more realistic situation that shows how the two people are alike in interests.

4. **Incorporating Real-Life Dynamics:**

- If the idea makes valid points, use the way your real-life group of friends interacts in the story. The interactions and development of the plot are affected by these dynamics in what ways?

5. **Balancing Roles**:

- Make sure that each character is important to the story. Even if some characters are more important than others, they should all be important to the story in some way.

6. **Respecting Boundaries**:

- Keep an eye on your friends' limits. You shouldn't include private or sensitive information unless they have given you permission to do so.

7. **Collaborative Story Arcs**:

- Structure your stories in a way that lets the characters work together and talk to each other. What happens to each of their stories when they join together?

8. **Review and Feedback**:

- Talk about the story with your friends every so often. Are they happy with how their character is portrayed and where the story is going? Be ready to make changes based on what they say.

9. **Resolving the Plot**:

- As you get closer to the end of the story, make sure that each character's arc ends in a way that fits with the overall plot.

10. **Celebrating the Finished Story**:

- When you're done with the story, send it to your friends. You could hold a special reading session or make a small booklet to keep.

CHAPTER **88**

STORY PROMPT JAR

Objective:

D RAW STORY IDEAS FROM a jar and have people add to it to encourage creativity and spontaneity in their writing.

Guidelines:

1. **Preparing the Jar**:

   ○ Find a big, clear jar or box that has enough room for several sheets of paper. If you want, you can decorate the jar to make it look appealing and attractive.

2. **Gathering Supplies**:

   ○ Give them pens or pencils, small pieces of paper, or notecards to write on.

3. **Creating Prompts**:

   ○ Ask each participant to write down at least one idea for a story on one of the strips of paper. It could be a single word, an idea for a character, a setting, a situation, or even the first lines of a story.

4. **Mixing the Prompts**:

   ○ Each piece of paper should be folded in half and put in the jar. Somewhat shake the jar to mix everything well.

5. **Drawing Prompts**:

○ Each person should take a prompt from the jar. If the group is big, you might want to have a few people draw at a time to keep things moving.

6. **Writing Time**:

○ Schedule a certain amount of time to write. There are different options for this, from a short 10-minute writing session to a longer, more in-depth story session.

7. **Sharing Stories**:

○ Encourage people to share their stories with the group after they've written them. Individuals may choose not to do this if they are uncomfortable with sharing.

8. **Discussion and Feedback**:

○ After someone shares a story, give them time to get feedback and talk about it. Pay attention to what you liked about the story and what made it unique or interesting.

9. **Repeat and Rotate**:

○ If there's spare time, people can draw new prompts and write new stories, either at the same meeting or at a later one.

10. **Storage and Reuse**:

○ Remember to save the jar for future use. Every time, you can change the prompts to keep the game interesting.

CHAPTER 89

MEMORIES OF OUR PLACE

Objective:

W RITE A STORY SET in a place that is important to you and your friends. Include parts of your shared experiences, the unique features of the place, and a made-up plot.

Guidelines:

1. **Vivid Description of the Setting**:

   - Start by giving a detailed description of where the story takes place. For you and your friends, what makes this place unique? Sights, sounds, smells, and textures are all important for making everything come alive.

2. **Introducing Characters**:

   - Make characters that are based on you and your friends. You can make them up, but give them traits, quirks, or inside jokes that are true to your real-life relationships.

3. **Incorporating Shared Memories**:

   - Add things from the memories you both have of this place. It could be certain memories, traditions, or feelings that are linked to the place.

4. **Developing the Plot**:

- Write a story whose plot is not based on your real life but is affected by the surroundings you spent time in. The story could be about a mystery, an adventure, a party, or a problem that the characters have to solve.

5. Character Interactions and Dynamics:

- Check out how the characters talk to each other and affect each other. How do they remind you of the friends you have in real life? Adding both positive and negative aspects will give the relationships more depth.

6. Conflict or Challenge:

- Add a problem or conflict that the characters have to deal with. This should be at the heart of the story and require people to work together, solve problems, or grow.

7. Incorporating Elements of the Setting:

- Make use of the context in your story. What effect does the atmosphere have on the characters' actions, the plot's development, or how the conflict is solved?

8. Moments of Reflection and Bonding:

- Include moments when the characters think or connect that show how important the place is to them. How does their connection to the place help them get to know each other better or make their friendship stronger?

9. Climactic Moment:

- Build up to a huge moment that connects the scene, the characters, and the story. You should feel like this moment is important and fits with the spirit of the place.

10. Concluding Reflections:

- End the story with the characters thinking about what they've been through. After spending time in this special place, what did they learn or gain?

CHAPTER 90

HARMONY IN VERSES

Objective:

M AKE A POEM TOGETHER, with each person adding a line or verse and building on what has been said before to make a complete and powerful work.

Guidelines:

1. **Decide the Format and Theme**:

   ○ Choose the type of poem (free verse, rhymed, haiku, etc.) and its subject as a group. The theme doesn't have to be specific; it can be something broad like nature, feelings, or an experience.

2. **Starting the Poem**:

   ○ Someone should write the first line or stanza. The theme and mood of the poem should be set in this first line.

3. **Adding Contributions**:

   ○ Next, have each person add their own line or stanza. Each new part should add to the ones that came before it, keeping the poem's flow and main idea.

4. **Encourage Varied Perspectives**:

   ○ Insist that each contribution can show the person's voice or point of view, giving the poem more depth and richness.

5. Maintaining Cohesion:

- ○ Even if you use different voices, make sure the poem still flows well. Each line, or stanza, should be related to the theme and the lines that came before it in some way.

6. Refrain from Critique During Creation:

- ○ Don't criticize each other's work during the first round of writing. Try to build on the ideas of each other.

7 Review and Refine:

- ○ After everyone has added something, read the poem aloud. Talk about which lines or stanzas need to be improved for clarity, flow, or continuity.

8. Edit Collaboratively:

- ○ Make changes together, making sure that the changes honor what each person actually intended.

9. Celebrate and Share:

- ○ Once it's done, celebrate the work you all did together. You could share the poem online, at a reading, or in a public place.

10. Reflect on the Experience:

- ○ Think about how collaborative writing works. Talk about what you liked, what was hard, and what you learned from how the other person came up with their ideas.

CHAPTER 91

GALACTIC GOURMET: AN ALIEN COOKING SHOW

Objective:

W RITE UP WITH A humorous and crazy story about an alien who hosts a cooking show where the recipes are strange, exotic, and funny but not safe for humans to eat.

Guidelines:

1. **Introducing the Alien Host:**

   ○ Bring up the alien host of the cooking show to begin. Give them a name and a personality that are as unique as the food they make. In a funny and strange way, describe how they look.

2. **Setting Up the Cooking Show:**

   ○ Get ready for the cooking show. Is it sent all the way across the galaxy? How does the alien kitchen look? Make the setting as strange and out of place as the host.

3. **First Recipe Disaster:**

   ○ Get started with the first recipe, which should be funny because it's not good for people. This could include strange ingredients, weird ways of cooking, or results that you don't like. Like "Meteorite Meatballs" or "Nebula Noodles."

4. Audience Reaction:

- Include reactions from a variety of people, such as people who are confused, amused, or horrified by the food. The way they react should make it funnier.

5. Cooking Show Challenges:

- Create issues or obstacles that happen on the show. Perhaps an object floats away in the absence of gravity, or the alien host creates a miniature black hole by accident.

6. More Outlandish Recipes:

- Keep going with more recipes that are obviously not edible. With things like "alien tentacles" or "comet dust" in them, each dish should be stranger than the last.

7. Cultural Misunderstandings:

- Use cultural misunderstandings to your advantage between the alien host and the people who watch them. The host might get people's tastes in food wrong in a funny way.

8. Climactic Culinary Creation:

- Build up to an ultimate recipe that is the craziest thing about the show. This dish should be the most ridiculously awful to eat yet, which will make the ending funny.

9. Wrap-Up and Sign-Off:

- At the end of the show, let the alien host sign off in their own unique way, not caring if the humans are shocked or upset.

10. Reflective Ending:

- Wrap up with a short human-centered thought about the show. It could be a funny review, a post on social media, or a conversation between viewers about the weird world of alien food.

CHAPTER 92

THE TIME-TRAVELING HAIRDRESSER

Objective:

WRITE AN ENTERTAINING TALE about a hairdresser who accidentally learns how to travel through time while cutting hair, giving people from times past crazy, out-of-date hairstyles.

Guidelines:

1. **Introducing the Hairdresser:**

   ○ Start by introducing the main character, a skilled hairdresser who doesn't know what's going on. Give them a unique personality and a desire to try out new, daring hairstyles.

2. **Discovery of Time Travel:**

   ○ Describe how the hairdresser finds out about time travel accidentally. It might happen when they use a certain mix of hair products or a certain way to cut their hair.

3. **First Accidental Time Jump:**

   ○ Write down the first time jump. The hairdresser could suddenly find themselves in the past, like in ancient Egypt or Europe in the Middle Ages, with scissors in hand.

4. Historical Figure's Encounter:

- ○ Have the hairdresser meet a historical figure who wants a haircut because they are interested or amused. The figure should get a hairstyle that is totally out of place for their time, like a punk mohawk or a neon-dyed bob, after this event.

5. Confusion and Humor:

- ○ Add humor by showing how the historical figure reacts to their new hairstyle and how it confuses people of the time.

6. Series of Time Jumps:

- ○ Keep going with a series of random time jumps that each lead to a funny interaction with a different historical figure and a crazy hairstyle.

7. Impact on History:

- ○ Look into the funny ways that these hairstyles can be used to describe historical events. How do these old styles change how people think about these characters?

8. Quest to Return Home:

- ○ Add a subplot where the hairdresser tries to figure out how to control their time-traveling power so they can get back home. They could get advice from scientists or inventors from the past.

9. Climactic Haircut:

- ○ Build up to a significant haircut that holds the key to getting back to their own time. This could be about a famous historical figure or a momentous event in history.

10. Return and Resolution:

- ○ At the end, have the hairdresser go back to their own time, maybe leaving behind a history of strange hairstyles. How have their travels changed the way they think about history and hairdressing?

11. **Reflective Ending**:

- When the story ends, the hairdresser is back at the salon, thinking about how amazing their journey was. Since they now understand how important their work is, they might keep their time-traveling adventures a secret.

CHAPTER 93

DINO DAY AT SCHOOL

Objective:

WRITE AN AMUSING AND lighthearted story about a teenager who brings their pet dinosaur to school. The dinosaur turns out to be the class clown and causes a lot of funny things to happen.

Guidelines:

1. **Introduction of Teen and Dinosaur:**

   ○ Continue by introducing the main character, a teen, and their strange pet dinosaur. How did they get a dinosaur as a pet? Who is the dinosaur and what is its name?

2. **Arrival at School:**

   ○ Describe what happens when they bring the dinosaur to school. Record how the students and teachers react when they see a dinosaur come into the school.

3. **First Classroom Shenanigans:**

   ○ Start with the first classroom scene, where the dinosaur's naughty side is shown. In class, the dinosaur might try to answer a question with a loud roar or draw on the board with its tail.

4. **Lunchtime Mayhem:**

- Come up with something humorous to do during lunchtime. The dinosaur might eat someone's homework by mistake, thinking it was lunch, or it might chase a soccer ball around for fun, which would stop a game.

5. The Dinosaur in Gym Class:

- Think about how crazy things would be if the dinosaur went to gym class. What about its size and strength makes a simple game a hilarious mess?

6. Science Lab Experiment:

- Add a scene in the science lab where the dinosaur's interest leads to something strange, like mixing chemicals by accident, which has a funny effect.

7. Classmates' Reactions:

- Show a variety of responses from your classmates. Some people might find the dinosaur's behaviors funny, while others might find them annoying or confusing.

8. Teachers' Attempts to Maintain Order:

- Describe how the teachers attempted to keep order and discipline in the classroom while a class clown dinosaur was present.

9. Turning Chaos into a Lesson:

- A creative teacher could use the dinosaur's antics to teach about dinosaurs, prehistoric times, or how important it is to treat all of your classmates with respect, even if they are from the Cretaceous period.

10. Concluding the School Day:

- Include the end of the school day. To what extent has the dinosaur's presence turned a normal day into an unforgettable event?

11. Reflections on Friendship and Acceptance:

- At the end, have the teen think back on the day and the lessons they learned about friendship, acceptance, and how fun it is to have a dinosaur at school.

CHAPTER 94

MAYOR BARKLEY'S TOWN

Objective:

WRITE AN ENTERTAINING AND lighthearted story about a town whose mayor is a talking dog who is known for making laws that are hard to understand, like making cats wear hats and requiring them to take naps.

Guidelines:

1. **Introduction of Mayor Barkley:**

    ○ Start by talking about Mayor Barkley, the dog. Explain what kind of person they are, what breed they are, and how they became mayor. What do the people in the town like about them?

2. **Depicting the Town:**

    ○ Give an overview of how the town looked when Mayor Barkley was in charge. In what ways is it different or funny? How do the people of the town get used to having a dog as mayor?

3. **Absurd Laws and Regulations:**

    ○ List some of the most silly and funny laws that Mayor Barkley has made. Explain the (il)logic behind laws that say cats can't wear hats, that say people have to take naps, and maybe that say people have to rub their cats' bellies every day.

4. Townspeople's Reactions and Adaptations:

- Show how different people in the town reacted. What do they think of Mayor Barkley's rules? Include scenes where people in the area find funny ways to get around the laws or get around them in some way.

5. A Day in the Life of Mayor Barkley:

- Explain what a typical day for Mayor Barkley looks like. Describe the dog mayor's official duties, interactions with people in the town, and how he or she runs the town's business.

6. Challenge or Conflict:

- Make the town face a problem or conflict. There might be a competition for mayor between cats, or one of Mayor Barkley's laws might be in question.

7. Mayor Barkley's Solutions:

- Show how Mayor Barkley solves problems in a creative way. How does their dog's point of view help them find creative and funny solutions?

8. Community Events:

- Include a community event that shows how quirky the town is. Maybe a festival for dogs with games and activities that follow Mayor Barkley's rules.

9. Townspeople's Support and Love:

- Even though it's silly, show how much the people of the town really love and support Mayor Barkley. What good things has the dog mayor done for the community?

10. Concluding with a Barkley Address:

- At the end, have Mayor Barkley speak to the town, maybe at a community event. What wise words (or funny dog jokes) do they share?

11. Reflection on Unity and Joy:

- Mayor Barkley and the people of the town should both talk about how happy and united they are that there is a talking dog as mayor at the end of the story.

CHAPTER 95

THE MISADVENTURES OF INVENTOR IZZIE

Objective:

WRITE AN FUNNY TALE about an inventor whose inventions always work backwards, which causes a lot of funny and strange things to happen.

Guidelines:

1. **Introduction of the Inventor**:

   ○ Inventor Izzie is the main character. She is a good-hearted but often unsuccessful inventor. Describe their personality, their desire to create new things, and how they stay positive even though bad things happen all the time.

2. **Showcasing the Inventions**:

   ○ Izzie should start by showing off a new invention, like a vacuum cleaner that is supposed to be the best cleaner ever, only to find that it throws dirt away instead of sucking it in.

3. **Community Responses**:

   ○ Write about how people around Izzie, like her neighbors, friends, and family, reacted to these inventions. Add a mix of amusement, frustration, and confusion over Izzie's gadgets that work backwards.

4. A Series of Inventive Failures:

- Izzie is still making a bunch of gadgets, and each one has an ironic twist. A car that can only go backwards, a clock that works backwards, or a toaster that freezes bread instead of toasting it.

5. Izzie's Optimism and Determination:

- Even though she has failed, show how determined and optimistic Izzie is. Display how they keep going back to the drawing board, not giving up.

6. An Unexpected Success:

- Create a scenario in where one of Izzie's broken inventions saves the day out of the blue. Someone might avoid an accident because the clock is running backwards, or a burglar might be scared off by the vacuum's noise.

7. Community's Appreciation:

- After the unexpected success, show how people start to value Izzie's inventions in their own special way. They may begin to discover funny or unusual ways to use the gadgets.

8. Izzie's Realization:

- Make Izzie realize that success can appear in strange ways. Even though the inventions don't do what they're supposed to, they still make people happy and useful in other ways.

9. A Grand Invention Event:

- Build up to a town event where Izzie's inventions will be shown off, and enjoy how weird and old-fashioned they are.

10. Concluding with Acceptance and Joy:

- Izzie should feel happy and appreciated by the end. Remember the message that it's okay if things don't go as planned and that there is joy in becoming flawed.

CHAPTER 96

THE WIZARD'S APPRENTICE

Objective:

C REATE A WHIMSICAL AND entertaining story about a wizard's apprentice who tries to cast spells but is always clumsy and fails hilariously.

Guidelines:

1. **Introduction of the Apprentice:**

   ○ Start by introducing the trainee, a character who really wants to learn how to be a wizard but always seems to get spells wrong. What kind of person are they? Are they too eager, forgetful, or just unlucky?

2. **The Wizard Mentor:**

   ○ Describe the apprentice's teacher, a wise wizard who tries to teach the apprentice how to do magic right. How do they feel about each other? Is the mentor patient or getting frustrated?

3. **First Spell Gone Wrong:**

   ○ Start with the apprentice's first big mistake with magic. They might try a simple spell that goes horribly wrong. For instance, a spell that cleans and turns everything upside down.

4. **Escalating Magical Disasters:**

- Keep going with a series of magical failures that get worse. Every time they try to cast a spell, something even stranger and funnier should happen. Maybe a spell that makes clothes invisible or a spell that makes things fly and dance around without being able to stop them.

5. Reactions of Those Around:

- Include how the characters around the apprentice feel. How do other apprentices, magical beings, or people in the town react to these disasters caused by spells?

6. A Critical Challenge:

- Draw up a serious issue that the apprentice needs to solve with magic. It's tough out there, and everyone thinks another disaster is going to happen.

7. Turning Point:

- Set up a turning point where the apprentice's mistake solves the problem or helps in a way that wasn't expected. Maybe a failed spell stops a bad guy or solves a problem that has been going on for a long time.

8. Growth and Self-Acceptance:

- Show how the apprentice has grown by showing what they've done. How do they come to a point where they accept the way they do magic?

9. The Mentor's Wisdom:

- Have the mentor give the apprentice some advice, pointing out that their methods aren't typical but that they have their own kind of magic.

10. Concluding with a New Outlook:

- At the end, have the apprentice embrace their own unique magic style. Even though they're not very good at spells, they've found a way to use magic to help them.

11. Reflection on Uniqueness and Creativity:

- At the end, think about how important it is to accept your own uniqueness and how inspiration can come from the strangest places.

CHAPTER 97

THE UNFORTUNATE WEATHER OF WALTER

Objective:

W RITE SOMETHING HUMOROUS ABOUT a character who is followed by a mischievous cloud that rains on them when they are doing something embarrassing. This causes a series of funny and awkward situations.

Guidelines:

1. **Character Introduction**:

   ○ Bring the protagonist, Walter. Who finds themselves in awkward situations. Describe their personality. Are they awkward, unlucky, or just a normal person with a strange problem?

2. **The Mischievous Cloud's Appearance**:

   ○ Describe the first time you saw the evil cloud. How does Walter feel when he learns that it rains on him when he's being silly?

3. **Series of Embarrassing Incidents**:

   ○ Make up some embarrassing events for Walter. Every event should be funnier than the last, like spilling coffee on a crush or tripping in public, and then it should rain from the sky.

4. Walter's Attempts to Cope:

- Show various methods that Walter has tried to deal with or trick the cloud. This could mean carrying an umbrella around with him all the time, staying inside, or finding humor in his situation.

5. Public Reactions and Adaptation:

- Describe how the people around Walter reacted. What do his family, friends, and strangers think about his personal raincloud? Does Walter become famous or just weird in the area?

6. The Cloud's Personality:

- Keep the cloud have its own personality. Does it look like it enjoys Walter's bad luck, or does it not care? It might be a little naughty sometimes.

7. Moment of Realization:

- Have an impact on Walter's understanding. Do you think he figures out why the cloud is acting that way? Or does he look at his embarrassing moments in a new way?

8. Turning the Situation Around:

- Show how Walter makes the best of his situation with the cloud. Possibly, he uses it to break the ice with new people or discovers a way to assist others with his very special friend.

9. Climactic Event:

- Build up to an immense occurrence that changes how Walter feels about the cloud. This could be a big event in someone's life or a big act of kindness that changes how the cloud acts.

10. Resolution and Acceptance:

- Finish with Walter figuring out how to get along with the cloud. How does he accept his strange fate? In what ways has he grown and learned to accept himself?

11. **Reflective Ending**:

- Walter should think about his trip with the cloud at the end. How has this strange event changed his view on life and his ability to deal with being embarrassed?

CHAPTER 98

VEGGIE UPRISING

Objective:

I MAGINE AN FUNNY AND unrealistic world where vegetables are intelligent and plan a funny revolt against being eaten by people.

Guidelines:

1. **World Where Vegetables are Alive:**

   ○ Begin by making a world where vegetables can feel things. Describe their society, how they interact with each other, and how they see people.

2. **Introduction of Vegetable Characters:**

   ○ Bring in some important vegetable characters, each with their own personality. A brave carrot leader, a wise old potato, or a group of peas who don't want to follow the rules.

3. **Discovery of Their Fate:**

   ○ Have the vegetables find out that they will be eaten in the end. This information can come from overhearing a conversation, reading a leaflet, or spotting a TV ad.

4. **Planning the Uprising:**

   ○ Describe how the vegetables plan to rise up. They should come up with

funny and unusual plans, like hiding, holding a march in the fridge, or
making a scene in the kitchen to keep them busy.

5. Comical Attempts to Avoid Being Eaten:

- Include footage of the vegetables' funny attempts to stay alive. These could
include getting out of the salad bowl, tickling people's noses to keep them
from getting chopped, or pretending to be things that aren't food.

6. Humans' Reactions:

- Show how the people in the world react to these strange events. The people
could be confused, amused, or completely unaware that the vegetables could
feel things.

7. Misadventures and Mishaps:

- Make the vegetables go through a bunch of different incidents and adventures along the way. They might fight over fruit or have a pet that gets in the
way of their plans.

8. The Climactic Showdown:

- Build up to a major battle, maybe in a grocery store or a kitchen, where the
vegetables make their last stand. This can include funny lines of dialogue
and silly situations.

9. Peaceful Resolution:

- Come up with a peaceful and funny way to end. People and vegetables might
understand each other, or the vegetables might realize they have a purpose
in the world other than being eaten.

10. Reflections on the Adventure:

- At the end, have the vegetables think about their trip. What have they
learned about whom they are, where they belong, and how they see people?

11. The New Status Quo:

○ Describe the new way things are. How do the vegetables live with people now that they've risen? What changes in their world and how people treat them?

CHAPTER 99

URBAN PIRATES OF THE ASPHALT SEA

Objective:

C OME UP WITH A silly and interesting story about a group of pirates who ride around cities in a ship on wheels and steal from fast food restaurants and supermarkets for fun.

Guidelines:

1. **Introduction of the Pirate Crew:**

   o Start by telling us about the charming pirate crew and their leader. Describe their personalities, the clothes they wear in cities, and their ship that has wheels.

2. **The Ship on Wheels:**

   o Draw a clear picture of their ship on wheels. How is it designed to get around in city streets? What strange changes does it make for sailing in cities?

3. **First Plundering Adventure:**

   o Start with the first time the crew went on a stealth mission. They might buy burgers and fries at a fast food place or snacks and soda at a grocery store.

4. **Reactions from Locals and Authorities:**

- Show how the people and authorities in the area responded to these strange pirates. Does it make them laugh, make sense, or do they join in the fun?

5. Pirate Code and Ethics:

- Establish that the pirates have morals, even though they steal. Others might be shockingly nice, pay for what they take, or do good things along the way.

6. Encounters with Rival Crews:

- Introduce rival urban pirate crews, each with their own unique vehicles. This will cause funny fights and races through the city.

7. Treasure Hunt in the City:

- Send the pirates through the city on a treasure hunt. The "treasure map" could be a funny take on a GPS or city guide.

8. Challenges and Escapades:

- Describe the problems and adventures they face, such as figuring out how to get through traffic, misunderstanding street signs, or dealing with a parrot that sounds like a car alarm.

9. Community Impact:

- Show how the pirates make the community better. They might find a lost child or stop a crime without meaning to.

10. Climactic Showdown:

- Build up to a final showdown with a rival crew or a misunderstanding with the police that is solved in a fun and calm way.

11. Legacy of the Urban Pirates:

- At last, talk about what the pirates leave behind in the city. They might become legends in the area, leading to pirate-themed events or community get-togethers.

12. **Reflective Ending**:

- End with the crew setting sail (or rolling away) on their next adventure while they think about their unique way of life and the bonds they've made.

CHAPTER 100

CIRCUS OF THE CIRCUIT

Objective:

I MAGINE A FUN AND creative story about a group of robots who leave their dull factory life to follow their dream of becoming circus performers. The story should explore themes of freedom, ambition, and the joy of performance.

Guidelines:

1. **Introduction of the Robots**:

   ○ Start by setting the story in a factory with the robot characters. What do they do at the factory? Why do they want something more exciting and satisfying in their mechanical lives?

2. **The Dream of the Circus**:

   ○ Show how the robots decide they want to join the circus. They might see a circus poster or hear someone talking about how magical the circus is.

3. **Planning the Escape**:

   ○ Describe how they plan to get out of the factory. To do this, they might need to use smart strategies to get around security systems or get help from a kind person.

4. **The Great Escape**:

○ Tell us about their brave escape. The trip from the factory to the circus can be funny and dangerous at the same time.

5. **First Encounter with the Circus**:

○ Highlight their first experience with the circus and the performers. What do the robots think of this exciting new world? What do the human performers think of them?

6. **Learning the Art of Performance**:

○ Describe how the robots are learning different circus acts. Every robot might be good at something different, like acrobatics, juggling, or clowning.

7. **Overcoming Setbacks**:

○ Include setbacks or difficulties on their way to becoming performers. Possible reasons for this are technical problems, doubts from experienced performers, or the fear of being sent back to the factory.

8. **Debut Performance**:

○ Get ready for the robots' first performance. The act should be a creative mix of the mechanical skills they already have and the circus skills they have recently learned.

9. **Audience's Reaction**:

○ Describe how the audience responded. The robots might have a one-of-a-kind show that makes people love them and gets them a permanent spot in the circus.

10. **Reflection on Their New Lives**:

○ At the end, have the robots think about their new lives. What are the differences between them now and when they left the factory? What does it mean to them to be in the circus?

11. **New Aspirations**:

○ Finally, give a hint at what the robots might want to do next now that they've reached their first big goal.

CHAPTER 101

SPACE SHENANIGANS: THE CLASS TRIP

Objective:

WRITE AN IMAGINATIVE AND amusing story about a school class that goes on a field trip to space and has a bunch of strange and funny things happen, like meeting a planet made of bouncy castles and sandwiches that float in the air.

Guidelines:

1. **Introduction of the Class and Setting**:

   ○ Start by informing the class about their teacher. Set the mood for how excited they are about the field trip to another galaxy. What futuristic or fantastical parts do they have in their world?

2. **Blast Off and Initial Mishap**:

   ○ Outline the rocket launch and the first problem that happened. Maybe there is no gravity, so everyday things like sandwiches float around the spaceship all over the place.

3. **Arrival at the First Destination**:

   ○ As soon as the class gets to their first spot, like a planet or space station, something silly but harmless should happen. They might meet a creature in space that talks through dance or a planet where the ground is as springy as a trampoline.

4. Series of Whimsical Events:

○ Make up a string of silly and funny events. This could mean going to a planet made of bouncy castles, a space museum where holographic versions of historical figures come to life, or a nebula that sings.

5. Students' and Teacher's Reactions:

○ Show how the students and teacher reacted in different ways. Some people might find the strange things exciting, others might find them hilariously overwhelming, and still others might, surprisingly, get used to them.

6. Educational Yet Funny Moments:

○ With a funny twist, include educational parts in the crazy stuff, like learning about gravity, space phenomena, or alien cultures.

7. A Minor Crisis:

○ Create a tiny issue that needs to be solved. For example, the spaceship could get stuck in a cosmic jelly or they could take a wrong turn at an asteroid belt.

8. Students Saving the Day:

○ Let the students save the day by working together, using their wit, or using what they've learned about space.

9. Return Journey:

○ Describe their way back. What do they learn or find funny about their trip? Is there a surprise in space at the last minute?

10. Reflections on the Trip:

○ At the end, have the class think about their interstellar field trip. How has the experience brought them closer together, and what crazy stories do they have to share?

11. Teaser for Future Trips:

- ○ Finish off with a hint about the next field trip they might go on. There might be a story about an adventure that takes place in the past or a trip to the center of the Earth.

ALSO BY JEFFREY C. CHAPMAN

Adulting Hard for Young Men

Adulting Hard for Young Women

Adulting Hard After College

Adulting Hard in Your Late Twenties and Thirties

Adulting Hard For Couples

Adulting Hard for New Parents

Adulting Hard as an Introvert or Highly Sensitive Person

Adulting Hard and Laughing Harder

Adulting Hard: Life Skills for Teens

101 Self-Care Activities

101 Writing Prompts for Kids

Made in the USA
Columbia, SC
17 December 2024

49738775R00126